The Retirement & Legacy Blueprint™

How to Achieve Clarity, Confidence, and Comfort
in Retirement and Beyond

Christopher J. Berry, JD, CELA®, CFP®
Castle Wealth Group

CHRISTOPHER J. BERRY, JD, CELA®, CFP® | Castle Wealth Group
1024 E. Grand River Ave., Suite A
Brighton, Michigan 48116
www.CastleWealthGroup.com
www.MichiganEstatePlanning.com

Book layout ©2022 Advisors Excel, LLC

THE RETIREMENT & LEGACY BLUEPRINT™
CHRISTOPHER J. BERRY, JD, CELA®, CFP®

ISBN 9798499908426

Christopher J. Berry, JD, CELA®, CFP® is registered as an Investment Advisor Representative and is a licensed insurance agent in the states of Michigan, South Carolina, Florida, and Georgia. Castle Wealth Group is an independent financial services firm that helps individuals create retirement strategies using a variety of investment and insurance products to custom suit their needs and objectives. In addition to his financial firm, Christopher Berry is a Certified Elder Law Attorney and runs Castle Wealth Group Legal, which is an Estate Planning and Elder Law firm that helps build legal structures to protect everything clients have worked so hard to build.

The contents of this book are provided for informational purposes only and are not intended to serve as the basis for any financial decisions. Any tax, legal, or estate planning information is general in nature. It should not be construed as legal or tax advice. Always consult an attorney or tax professional regarding the applicability of this information to your unique situation.

Information presented is believed to be factual and up-to-date, but we do not guarantee its accuracy, and it should not be regarded as a complete analysis of the subjects discussed. All expressions of opinion are those of the author as of the date of publication and are subject to change. Content should not be construed as personalized investment advice nor should it be interpreted as an offer to buy or sell any securities mentioned. A financial advisor should be consulted before implementing any of the strategies presented.

Investing involves risk, including the potential loss of principal. No investment strategy can guarantee a profit or protect against loss in periods of declining values. Any references to protection benefits or guaranteed/lifetime income streams refer only to fixed insurance products, not securities or investment products. Insurance and annuity product guarantees are backed by the financial strength and claims-paying ability of the issuing insurance company.

We are an independent financial services firm helping individuals create retirement strategies using a variety of investment and insurance products to custom suit their needs and objectives. Investment advisory services offered only by duly registered individuals through AE Wealth Management, LLC (AEWM) and Castle Wealth Group are not affiliated companies.

Any names used in the examples in this book are hypothetical only and do not represent actual clients.

"It does not do to leave a live dragon out of your calculations if you live near one."

~ J.R.R. Tolkien

This book is dedicated to my son, Ryan, and daughter, Madison. The two of you are why I work so hard.

You make me strive to be better—a better father, attorney, advisor, author. . .a better person.

You are the future.

Thank you to my father, who gave me my constant intellectual curiosity. Thank you to my mom, who kept me grounded.

To Rochelle, thank you for being my partner and supporting our family every step of the way.

Table of Contents

The Importance of Planning

"Give me six hours to chop down a tree and I will spend the first four sharpening the ax."
— Abraham Lincoln

If you've ever planned a trip with your family, you probably started by asking a lot of questions. "Where do we want to go?" "What do we want to do?" "How much is it going to cost?" Once you found the answers, you might have prepared an itinerary.

The Oxford dictionary defines an itinerary as "a planned route or journey."

Life after work is also a journey—one most of us look forward to. Unfortunately, some of us spend more time preparing for a one-week trip than we do for decades of retirement.

This idea came to me while sitting in the large conference room of my office. Together with my wife, my parents, and our two children—Ryan, then six, and Madison, four—we gathered there to plan our first trip to Disney World.

Discussing a Disney vacation seemed sensible. After all, it's a busy place with endless attractions and a sea of customers. With so much to choose from, each of us had different boxes we wanted to check, but like everything else we'd done as a family, there would have to be some give and take. In considering the importance each attraction held for us and the physical distances between them, plenty of questions got raised. As you can imagine, each family member had details they wanted to work out before our arrival:

- Which parks would we visit and on which days?
- Which "Fast Passes" would we need for the rides we wanted to ride?
- Which restaurants had the menu items appealing to all our tastes?
- How much walking would we have to do?

It was a grueling experience to say the least. The conference room looked more like a campsite than a meeting space, but after five hours and a lot of empty food containers, we emerged from that room with a plan.

We had carefully considered our individual preferences, prioritized them, and felt prepared for whatever Disney might throw at us. If time permitted, maybe we'd be able to do more, but if a ride was closed or the weather turned to rain: "no problem"—we wouldn't be standing around asking ourselves, "now what?" The planning we did would give us options.

We wanted our kids to remember "that amazing trip" and not "that time we showed up too late for the tour." I'd rather hear them recount all the "bad dad jokes," as they call them, and not our big plans that fell through. The latter might have been the case had we "winged it."

Vacation planning makes sense. Retirement and legacy planning makes sense for the same reasons. Whether you're planning for one week or the next forty years, there are basic questions that need to be answered:

- What do we want to do?
- Where do we want to stay?
- How long will we stay there?
- What if our plans change?

And most importantly: How much will it all cost?

While retirement planning may not be as exciting as a trip to Magic Kingdom, both require planning. You only have one chance to "nail" your retirement -- you only have one chance to leave the legacy you want to leave.

For fifteen years, I've watched adult children clean up messes left by their parents. Whether they underestimated the significant cost of long-term care or burned through their savings, their children were left with no other choice but to make-up the shortcomings. Some scenarios had parents moving-in with their children, who were later left to deal with a messy probate process because no estate plan was ever formalized. This is not the legacy you want to leave.

Retirement is a different phase of life from your years spent working and it requires a different kind of strategy. Recognizing the differences is an important first step toward building a solid plan. We see two phases, one while you are working, which is the accumulation phase, and then retirement, which is the preservation and distribution phase.

Phase One – Accumulation
Building wealth is similar to climbing a mountain. By dedicating yourself to building the skills and putting in the hours, you finally made it to the top. All that work has given you the ability to rest now. This life phase was about accumulation or "building a nest egg."

Phase Two – Preservation and Distribution
If accumulation was your trip up the mountain, retirement should be the reward for reaching the top. Any direction you go from here should be easy. Gravity isn't bearing down like it once was -- right? Yes, this journey should feel easier, but it still requires navigation. It still takes planning.

Reaching the top means it's time to take a breath and reflect on what's next -- to realize a new phase of your life has begun. It's time to begin thinking about the preservation and distribution of your assets.

By building a Retirement and Legacy Blueprint, you can accomplish the "Three C's."

The Three C's

Protecting what you've accumulated and making it last (at least as long as you do) requires a different approach than the accumulation phase. The Retirement and Legacy Blueprint™ was designed by Castle Wealth Group, to help families achieve the "Three C's" in legal, financial, and tax planning strategies. The Three C's seek:

CLARITY

By creating a Retirement & Legacy Blueprint, families should **clearly** understand:

- What they are leaving to loved ones
- The legal tools that may be necessary to use
- Knowing they will achieve tax efficiency in retirement
- The circumstances that dictate the use of different accounts

CONFIDENCE

The Retirement & Legacy Blueprint™ is intended to help provide families complete **confidence** that their assets will efficiently transfer to the next generation.

COMFORT

Comfort means "having your ducks in a row." The Retirement & Legacy Blueprint™ harmonizes the following plans so they can work together:

- Income plan
- Investment plan
- Tax plan
- Health-care plan
- Legacy plan

Families experience a sense of **comfort** when their individual plans are effectively aligned to work together.

In my office, we refer to retirement planning as "planning for the second half of life." Life expectancies have increased to the point where a person may spend as much time in retirement as they spent working. Funding such a lengthy period from one's savings can be a scary thought. Financial advisors frequently hear their clients lament, "We wish we'd sat down with you five years ago."

The old adage "nothing is certain but death and taxes" is well known—still, much uncertainty remains. Maybe if the adage told us "when" and "how much" —then again. . .I'm not sure any of us want the answer to "when?" Answers to retirement and legacy questions don't crystallize on their own. And when we finally do get an answer to a question, it often leads to three new ones—too many unknowns can disrupt our peace of mind.

The unknown can sometimes be scary and some of us simply put our heads in the sand rather than preparing for "who knows what?" The best any of us can do is to "know that we can't know." Embracing this concept alone can be empowering.

We can drive ourselves crazy trying to answer "what might happen?" but the real question should be, "how do we prepare for it?" No one could predict the pandemic of 2020 or the extent of the market crash in 2008, but many who possess a proper financial plan likely experienced less stress and less anguish. Why? Because someone determined an appropriate mix of assets (or risk) designed to weather any type of storm—thus giving deference to the unknown.

"THE PROUD MAN CAN LEARN HUMILITY, BUT HE WILL BE PROUD OF IT."
- MIGNON MCLAUGHLIN

Who doesn't like to save a buck and look smart in the process? Sometimes those two things only happen when we defer to someone skilled in the art, which reminds me of a time early in our marriage when our dryer had stopped working. My wife and I were first-time homeowners, and I wanted to show her that not only was I book smart (and handsome), but handy as well.

Figuring I could learn what I needed to know by watching YouTube, I had completely dissected the issue in less than an hour. Or so I thought. Despite lacking the correct tools, I soon had the dryer taken apart, located the malfunctioning part, and placed an order for a new one online. A week later, now with the new part in hand, I switched it out and started putting the dryer back together.

But that's when I hit a snag. During the reassembly process, I heard a piece "snap" and thought to myself, "uh oh." As if that wasn't bad enough, I noticed still more pieces laying on the floor. "It can't be this hard," I thought.

Long story short, I had wasted countless hours, delayed having dry clothes for weeks, and now faced the unwanted task of consoling my wife, reminding her "at least I still had my good looks." Turns out, that wasn't cutting it, so I hustled out and purchased a new dryer. Imagine if I had just called a skilled repairman, I could have avoided a lot of frustration (not to mention a lot of wasted time and money), and we likely would have had dry clothes that day.

Answers to retirement and legacy questions don't crystallize on their own.

Many of us are afraid of the unknown, but I believe your concerns could be alleviated by constructing a Retirement & Legacy Blueprint. By doing so, you can find the necessary clarity to help manage long-term care risks, tax risks, and market volatility.

Your comfort in retirement and the legacy you leave for your loved ones can potentially improve when you work with someone experienced in coaching families during their transition from the accumulation phase to the preservation and distribution phase.

As practicing attorneys and financial advisors who are fiduciaries, we find ourselves held to the highest standard of care. Others are not always held to such a high standard, such as those solely offering the various products and tools you may or may not want. Think of the Fidelitys and Vanguards of the world, where they serve as a custodian while you pick your own investments.

We see this in the practice of law as well, where some attorneys prepare the same revocable trust for everyone, regardless of their specific needs. Another example of where you might see this is with annuity and insurance salespeople, who have limited access to products and solutions for their clients because they are only licensed to sell insurance and annuities.

Then there are portfolio managers, who mainly focus on managing assets. They often don't talk about the legal ramifications of how assets are held, nor do they offer tax planning advice. They may offer their clients some advice, but it may not be as comprehensive as that from a holistic planning firm.

On the other (positive) end of the spectrum, we have holistic advisors, whose approach entails looking at the entire puzzle, rather than a single piece. Legal, financial, and tax planning concepts are all pieces of the puzzle that must be correctly assembled in order to serve your best interests. By tying these areas together, holistic advisors can create comprehensive plans and not just an investment portfolio.

The experience possessed by the Castle Wealth Group team, and the current technology our company uses, enables us to develop a Retirement & Legacy Blueprint™, which addresses five key areas:

INCOME PLANNING
Our goal is to help ensure your expenses can be paid month to month with reliability and predictability for the rest of your life. This typically includes:

- Social Security Maximization
- Income & Expense Analysis
- An Inflation Plan
- A Spousal Plan
- A Written Income Plan

INVESTMENT PLANNING

Once your income plan is established, we will create an investment plan. This plan will be appropriate to your needs, goals, and tolerance for risk. These remaining assets, after income has been planned for, are assets that you do not need to draw from month to month. This typically includes:

- Assessing your Risk Tolerance
- Adjusting your portfolio to reduce fees
- Volatility Control
- An Evaluation of ways to reduce risk while still working towards your goals
- Longevity Protection

TAX PLANNING

Any comprehensive Retirement Plan will include a strategy for decreasing tax liabilities. This typically includes:

- Assessing the taxable nature of your current holdings
- Possible IRA Planning
- Strategizing ways to include tax-deferred or tax-free money in your plan
- Strategizing which tax category to draw income from first to potentially reduce the tax burden
- Discussing ways to leverage your qualified money to leave tax-free dollars to your beneficiaries

HEALTH CARE PLANNING

We will create a plan to help you address rising healthcare costs, while keeping your expense to a minimum, including:

- Looking at all aspects of Medicare, Parts A, B, and D

- Analyzing options for Long-Term Care Coverage

LEGACY PLANNING

It is important to ensure your hard-earned assets go to your beneficiaries in the most tax-efficient manner. As an estate planning attorney, I attempt to structure legacy plans designed to satisfy your desires and help safeguard against threats that taxes can pose for your loved ones. Our goal will be to help you:

- Maximize your estate and income tax planning opportunities
- Protect any assets in trust and ensure they are distributed to your beneficiary's probate-free
- Prevent your IRA and qualified accounts from becoming fully taxable to your beneficiaries upon your death

Having no retirement and legacy plan is like building a house with no blueprint—will it stand up to wind, rain, tornados, etc.? Likewise, will your plan be able to weather unnecessary taxes, market risk, and the potentially significant cost of long-term care? And how much stress caused by the probate process could be mitigated for your loved ones?

A Retirement & Legacy Blueprint™ can help you plan for whatever life may throw at you in retirement as you strive to gain the security, clarity, confidence, and comfort you deserve.

Within the pages of this book, I strive to explain concepts, strategies, rules, and regulations that factor into the pillars of retirement planning—income, investments, taxes, health care, and legacy.

CHAPTER 1
Longevity

"You know you're getting old when you stoop to tie your shoelaces and wonder what else you could do while you're down there."
— *George Burns*

I am going to live to 146. Go ahead, laugh. My kids do. I believe it, though. You might be asking how and where that number came from. Not sure, really.

I once attended a workshop where the presenter made important points regarding longevity.

First, medical technologies are advancing at an exponential pace, making it difficult to imagine what human life spans (even in our lifetimes) could become. Advancements in research may soon reverse cognitive decline in Alzheimer's patients and reduce the causal severity of cardiovascular and osteoporosis disease. Personally, I've had a total hip replacement at forty-one, which was unheard of just fifty years ago.

Second, staying in good health is largely affected by one's mindset. In my experience, the clients living "rich and rewarding" lives are the ones who always have something to look forward to doing. I've had eighty-year-old clients who volunteer in Haiti and clients in their nineties who still love to garden. One of my clients went skydiving for the first time on her eighty-fifth birthday. I truly believe we can find joy and extend our lives by pursuing new and exciting experiences.

It's about retiring to something, not retiring from something.

However, longevity can exacerbate the financial burden of long-term care or cause us to, unfortunately, run out of money.

You would think the prospect of the grave would loom more frightening as we age, yet many retirees say their number one fear is actually running out of money in their twilight years.[1] This fear is justified, in part, because of one significant factor: We're living longer.

According to the Social Security Administration, in 1950, the average life expectancy for a sixty-five-year-old man was seventy-eight, and the average for a sixty-five-year-old woman was eighty-one. In 2020, those averages were eighty-three and eighty-eight, respectively.[2]

The bottom line of many retirees' budget woes comes down to this: They just didn't plan to live so long. Now, when we are younger and in our working years, that's not something we necessarily see as a bad thing; don't some people fantasize about living forever or, at least, reaching the ripe old age of one hundred?

However, with a longer lifespan, as we near retirement, we face a few snags. Our resources are finite—we only have so much money to provide income—but our lifespans can be unpredictably long, perhaps longer than our resources allow. Also, longer lives don't necessarily equate with healthier lives. The longer you live, the more money you will likely need to spend on health care, even excluding long-term care needs like nursing homes.

You will also run into inflation. If you don't plan to live another twenty-five years but end up doing so, inflation at an

---

[1] Samiha Khanna. Journal of Accountancy. February 14, 2019. "Clients' Top Fear: Running out of Money."
https://www.journalofaccountancy.com/news/2019/feb/top-retirement-fears-201920387.html
[2] Social Security Administration. 2011 Trustees Report. "Actuarial Publications: Cohort Life Expectancy."
https://www.ssa.gov/OACT/TR/2011/lr5a4.html

average 2.5 percent will raise your $50,000-per-year budgeted need up to $93,000 per year. Or, if you live another eight years as inflation rises, you will need about $810,000 to cover those same expenses.[3] And this is before you count the expenses of any potential health care or long-term care needs.

Because we don't necessarily get to have our cake and eat it, too, our collective increased longevity hasn't necessarily increased the healthy years of our lives. Typically, our life-extending care most widely applies to the time in our lives where we will need more care in general. Think of common situations like a pacemaker at eighty-five, or cancer treatment at seventy-eight.

"Wow, Chris," I can hear you say. "Way to start with the good news first."

I know, I've painted a grim picture, but all I'm concerned about here is cost. It's hard to put a dollar sign on life, but that is essentially what we're talking about when discussing longevity and finances. According to the Stanford Center on Longevity, more than half of pre-retirees underestimate the life expectancy of the average sixty-five-year-old.[4] Living longer isn't a bad thing; it just costs more, and one key to a sound retirement strategy is preparing for it in advance.

One woman I know illustrates this picture perfectly. Her mother passed away in her late seventies after years of suffering from Alzheimer's disease and her father died at eighty from cancer.

With modern medicines and treatment, this woman was able to survive two rounds of breast cancer, manage her diabetes, and correct an irregular heart rhythm with a pacemaker, thus extending her life to age eighty-eight—nearly a decade beyond what she'd anticipated. Fortunately, she and her husband had

3 Katie Brockman. The Motley Fool. August 19, 2018. "More Americans are Living into Their 90s—and That's Bad News for Their Savings." https://www.fool.com/retirement/2018/08/19/more-americans-are-living-into-their-90s-and-thats.aspx
4 Stanford Center on Longevity. "Underestimating Years in Retirement." http://longevity.stanford.edu/underestimating-years-in-retirement/

saved and planned for a "just in case" scenario like this one. In addition to making preparations for the cost of assisted care and helping their children and grandchildren with their expenses, one of their "just-in-case" scenarios was living much longer than they anticipated. The last six years of her life were fraught with medical expenses, but she also felt blessed by the time she spent extending relationships with her children, grandchildren, and five great-grandchildren. She was able to pay her own medical expenses, including her final two years in a nursing home, making her twilight years truly golden.

In fact, she was more socially active with family and friends in her last three years than she'd been in the first four years after losing her husband. The planning she had done decades earlier allowed her to pass on a legacy to her children that was not only measurable in dollars, but by the rewarding time she spent with them.

Living longer can be so meaningful when you plan for your "just-in-cases."

Retiring Later

Planning for a long life in retirement partly depends on when you retire. While many people end up retiring earlier than they anticipated—due to injuries, layoffs, family crises, and other unforeseen circumstances—continuing to work past age sixty (and even sixty-five) is still a viable option for others and can be an excellent way to help establish financial comfort in retirement.

There are many reasons for this. For one, you obviously still earn a paycheck and the benefits accompanying it. Medical coverage and beefing up your retirement accounts with further savings can be significant by themselves but continuing your income also should keep you from dipping into your retirement funds, further allowing them the opportunity to grow.

Additionally, for many workers, their nine-to-five job is more than just clocking in and out. Having a sense of purpose can keep us active physically, mentally, and socially. That kind of activity and level of engagement may also help stave off many of the health problems that plague retirees. Avoiding a sedentary life is one of the advantages of staying plugged into the workforce, if possible.

My father was a professor and academic dean at a community college (and a basketball coach, too!) for forty-seven years. There was a running joke on campus that the professors were on the "carry out plan." Meaning they would work until they passed away. You may be asking why? It's not because they needed the money—back then, they had wonderful pensions.

The reason some professors worked into their eighties is they loved what they did, it was their passion and it energized them. Although the classes my dad taught routinely touched on the same material, each semester remained exciting. Watching new students express their thoughts and opinions while learning the evolving technology served to enhance his passion for teaching.

Using basketball as an example, rules changed, techniques changed, and even the level of athleticism rose. The 3-point shot, for example, changed coaching strategies and elevated the importance of court spacing and long-range shooting. The challenges presented to my father in the classroom and on the basketball court gave him even more incentive to stay and continue enjoying his chosen profession. It gave him something to look forward to, which is key to a healthy, happy retirement.

Health Care

Take a second to reflect on your health care plan. Although working up to or even past age sixty-five would allow you to avoid a coverage gap between your working years and Medicare, that may not be an option for you. Even if it is, when you retire, you will need to make some decisions about what kind of insurance coverage you may need to supplement your Medicare. Are there any medical needs you have that may require coverage in addition to Medicare? Did your parents or grandparents have any inherited medical conditions you might consider using a special savings plan to cover?

These are all questions that are important to review with your financial professional so you can be sure you have enough money put aside for health care.

Long-Term Care

Longevity means the need for long-term care is statistically more likely to happen. If you intend to pass on a legacy, planning for long-term care is paramount, since most estimates project nearly 70 percent of Americans will need some type of it.[5] However, this may be one of the biggest, most stressful pieces of longevity planning I encounter in my work. For one thing, who wants to talk about the point in their lives when they may feel the most limited? Who wants to dwell on what will happen if they no longer can toilet, bathe, dress, or feed themselves?

I get it; this is a less-than-fun part of planning. But a little bit of preparation now can go a long way!

When it comes to your longevity, just like with your goals, one of the important things to do is sit and dream. It may not be the fun, road-trip-to-the-Grand-Canyon kind of dreaming, but you can spend time envisioning how you want your twilight years to look.

For instance, if it is important for you to live in your home for as long as possible, who will provide for the day-to-day fixes and to-dos of housework if you become ill? Will you set aside money for a service, or do you have relatives or friends nearby whom you could comfortably allow to help you? Do you prefer in-home care over a nursing home or assisted living? This could be a good time to discuss the possibility of moving into a

---

[5] Moll Law Group. 2019. "The Cost of Long-Term Care." https://www.molllawgroup.com/the-cost-of-long-term-care.html

THE RETIREMENT AND LEGACY BLUEPRINT™ | 7

retirement community versus staying where you are or whether it's worth moving to another state and leaving relatives behind.

These are all important factors to discuss with your spouse and children, as *now* is the right time to address questions and concerns. For instance, is aging in place more important to one spouse than the other? Are the friends or relatives who live nearby emotionally, physically, and financially capable of helping you for a time if you face an illness?

Many families I meet with find these conversations very uncomfortable, particularly when children discuss nursing home care with their parents. A knee-jerk reaction for many is to promise they will care for their aging parents. This is noble and well-intentioned, but there needs to be an element of realism here. Does "help" from an adult child mean they stop by and help you with laundry, cooking, home maintenance, and bills? Or does it mean they move you into their spare room when you have hip surgery? Are they prepared to help you use the restroom and bathe if that becomes difficult for you to do on your own?

I don't mean to discourage families from caring for their own; this can be a profoundly admirable relationship when it works out. However, I've seen families put off planning for late-in-life care based on a tenuous promise that the adult children would care for their parents, only to watch as the support system crumbles. Sometimes this is because the assumed caregiver hasn't given serious thought to the preparation they would need, both in a formal sense and regarding their personal, physical, emotional, and financial commitments. This is often also because we can't see the future: Alzheimer's disease and other maladies of old age can exact a heavy toll. When a loved one reaches the point where he or she is at risk of wandering away or needs help with two or more activities of daily living, it can be more than one person or family can realistically handle.

If you know what you want, communicate with your family about both the best-case and worst-case scenarios. Then, hope for the best, and plan for the worst.

Realistic Cost of Care

Wrapped up in your planning should be a consideration for the cost of long-term care. Although many of us will need some degree of long-term care—including the 30 percent of us who may need up to five years of facility care—60 percent of us underestimate the costs of nursing home care. On average, consumers underestimate the annual cost of a private room in a nursing home by 51 percent.[6]

Another piece of planning for long-term care costs is anticipating inflation. It's common knowledge that prices have been and keep rising, which will lower your purchasing power on everything from food to medical care. Long-term care is a big piece of the inflation-disparity pie, which is part of why many find their estimates of nursing home care widely miss the mark. According to one survey, people expected to pay around $25,350 in annual out-of-pocket long-term care expenses, but, in reality, they'll more likely pay over $47,000.[7]

While local costs vary from state to state, here's the national median for various forms of long-term care (plus projections that account for a 3 percent annual inflation, so you can see what I'm talking about):[8]

[6] Tamara E. Holmes. Yahoo Finance. July 24, 2019. "Consumers Underestimate Costs of Long-Term Care."
https://finance.yahoo.com/news/consumers-underestimate-costs-long-term-173542918.html
[7] Moll Law Group. 2019. "The Cost of Long-Term Care."
https://www.molllawgroup.com/the-cost-of-long-term-care.html
[8] Genworth Financial. June 2018. "Cost of Care Survey 2018."
https://www.genworth.com/aging-and-you/finances/cost-of-care.html

Long-Term Care Costs: Inflation				
	Home Health Care, Homemaker Services	Adult Day Care	Assisted Living	Nursing Home (semi-private room)
Annual 2020	$54,912	$19,236	$51,600	$93,072
Annual 2030	$73,800	$25,848	$69,348	$125,076
Annual 2040	$99,180	$34,740	$93,192	$168,096
Annual 2050	$133,284	$46,692	$125,244	$225,912

Fund Your Long-Term Care

One critical mistake I see are those who haven't planned for long-term care because they assume the government will provide everything. But that's a big misconception. The government has two health insurance programs: Medicare and Medicaid. These can greatly assist you in your health care needs in retirement but usually don't provide enough coverage to cover all your health care costs in retirement. My firm isn't a government outpost, so we don't get to make decisions when it comes to forming policy and specifics about either one of these programs. I'm going to give the overview of both, but if you want to dive into the details of these programs, you can visit www.Medicare.gov and www.Medicaid.gov.

Medicare
Medicare covers those aged sixty-five and older and those who are disabled. Medicare's coverage of any nursing-home-related

health issues is limited. It might cover your nursing home stay if it is not a "custodial" stay, and it isn't long-term. For example, if you break a bone or suffer a stroke, stay in a nursing home for rehabilitative care, and then return home, Medicare may cover you. But, if you have developed dementia or are looking to move to a nursing facility because you can no longer bathe, dress, toilet, feed yourself, or take care of your hygiene, etc., then Medicare is not going to pay for your nursing home costs.[9]

Medicaid

Medicaid is a program the states administer, so funding, protocol, and limitations vary. Compared to Medicare, Medicaid more widely covers nursing home care, but it targets a different demographic: those with low incomes.

If you have more assets than the Medicaid limit in your state and need nursing home care, you will need to use those assets to pay for your care. You will also have a list of additional state-approved ways to spend some of these assets over the Medicaid limit, such as pre-purchasing burial plots and funeral expenses or paying off debts. After that, your remaining assets fund your nursing home stay until they are gone, at which point Medicaid will jump in.

Some people aren't stymied by this, thinking they will just pass on their financial assets early, gifting them to relatives, friends, and causes so they can qualify for Medicaid when they need it. However, to prevent this exact scenario, Uncle Sam has implemented the look-back period. Currently, if you enroll in Medicaid, you are subject to having the government scrutinize the last five years of your finances for large gifts or expenses that may subject you to penalties, temporarily making you ineligible for Medicaid coverage.

There are legal strategies to help preserve your assets when medical costs begin to skyrocket. One such strategy is to utilize an asset protection trust such as a Castle Trust™, a form of trust

---

[9] Medicare.gov. "What Part A covers." https://www.medicare.gov/what-medicare-covers/part-a/what-part-a-covers.html

that starts the clock running on the five-year Medicaid look-back period. Once five years have elapsed, everything inside the trust is protected from the nursing home and ensures that Medicaid spend-down rules are not violated.

In other words, Medicaid pays for a base level of care, leaving you with the resources needed to pay for additional services. This strategy can dramatically improve your quality of life and protect a healthy spouse from impoverishment.

So, if you're planning to preserve your money for future generations and retain control of your financial resources during your lifetime, you'll probably want to prepare for the costs of longevity beyond a "government plan." The following are additional options to fund long-term care costs.

Self-Funding

One way to fund a longer life is the old-fashioned way, through self-funding. There are a variety of financial tools you can use, and they all have their pros and cons. If your assets are in low-interest financial vehicles (savings, bonds, CDs), you risk letting inflation erode the value of your dollar. Or, if you are relying on the stock market, you have more growth potential, but you'll also want to consider the possible implications of market volatility. What if your assets take a hit? If you suffer a loss in your retirement portfolio in early or mid-retirement, you might have the option to "tighten your belt," so to speak, and cut back on discretionary spending to allow your portfolio the room to bounce back. But, if you are retired and depend on income from a stock account that just hit a downward stride, what are you going to do?

HSAs

These days, you might also be able to self-fund through a health savings account, or HSA, if you have access to one through a high-deductible health plan (you will not qualify to save in an HSA after enrolling in Medicare). In an HSA, any growth of your tax-deductible contributions will be tax-free, and any distributions paid out for qualified health costs are also tax-free. Long-term care expenses count as health costs, so, if this is an option available to you, it is one way to use the tax advantages to self-fund your longevity. Bear in mind, if you are younger than sixty-five, any money you use for nonqualified expenses will be subject to taxes and penalties, and, if you are older than sixty-five, any HSA money you use for non-medical expenses is subject to income tax.

LTCI

One slightly more nuanced way to pay for longevity, specifically for long-term care, is long-term care insurance, or LTCI. As car insurance protects your assets in case of a car accident and home insurance protects your assets in case something happens to your house, long-term care insurance aims to protect your assets in case you need long-term care in an at-home or nursing home situation.

As with other types of insurance, you will pay a monthly or annual premium in exchange for an insurance company paying for long-term care down the road. Typically, policies cover two to three years of care, which is adequate for an "average" situation: it's estimated 70 percent of Americans will need about three years of long-term care of some kind. However, it's important to consider you might not be "average" when you are preparing for long-term care costs; on average, 20 percent of today's sixty-five-year-olds could need care for longer than five years.[10]

Now, there are a few oft-cited components of LTCI that make it unattractive for some:

- Expense — LTCI can be expensive. It is generally less expensive the younger you are, but a fifty-five-year-old couple who purchased LTCI in 2022 could expect to pay $2,080 each year for an average three-year coverage

---

[10] David Levine. *U.S. News.* July 10, 2019. "How to Pay for Nursing home Costs." https://health.usnews.com/best-nursing-homes/articles/how-to-pay-for-nursing-home-costs

policy. And the annual cost only increases from there the older you are.[11]

- Limited options — Let's face it: LTCI may be expensive for consumers, but it can also be expensive for companies that offer it. With fewer companies willing to take on that expense, this narrows the market, meaning opportunities to price shop for policies with different options or custom benefits are limited.

- If you know you need it, you might not be able to get it — Insurance companies offering LTCI are taking on a risk that you may need LTCI. That risk is the foundation of the product—you may or may not need it. If you know you will need it because you have a dementia diagnosis or another illness for which you will need long-term care, you will likely not qualify for LTCI coverage.

- Use it or lose it—If you have LTCI and are in the minority of Americans who die having never needed long-term care, all the money you paid into your LTCI policy is gone.

- Possibly fluctuating rates—Your rate is not locked in on LTCI. Companies maintain the ability to raise or lower your premium amounts. This means some seniors face an ultimatum: Keep funding a policy at what might be a less affordable rate *or* lose coverage and let go of all the money they paid in so far.

After that, you might be thinking, "How can people possibly be interested in LTCI?" But let me repeat myself—as many as 70 percent of Americans will need long-term care. And, although only 8 percent of Americans have purchased LTCI, keep in mind the high cost of nursing home care. Can you afford $7,000 a month to put into nursing home care and still have

---

[11] American Association for Long-Term Care Insurance. January 12, 2021. "2022 National Long-Term Care Insurance Price Index." https://www.aaltci.org/long-term-care-insurance/learning-center/ltcfacts-2022.php

enough left over to protect your legacy? This is a very real concern: One study says 72 percent of Americans are impoverished by the end of just one year in a nursing home.[12] So, not to sound like a broken record, but it is vitally important to have a plan in place to deal with longevity and long-term care if you intend to leave a financial legacy.

A fundamental question to ask is whether long-term care insurance is necessary.

I am not a big fan of traditional LTCI because, in most cases, benefits can be achieved by implementing a proper legal strategy or by adding long-term benefits through a life insurance or annuity product rider.

Product Riders

LTCI and self-funding are not the only ways to plan for the expenses of longevity. Some companies are getting creative with their products, particularly insurance companies. One way they are retooling to meet people's needs is through optional product riders on annuities and life insurance. Elsewhere in this book, I talk about annuity basics, but here's a brief overview: Annuities are insurance contracts. You pay the insurance company a premium, either as a lump sum or as a series of payments over a set amount of time, in exchange for guaranteed income payments. One of the advantages of an annuity is it has access to riders, which allow you to tweak your contract for a fee, usually about 1 percent of the contract value annually. One annuity rider some companies offer is a long-term care rider. If you have an annuity with a long-term care rider and are not in need of long-term care, your contract behaves as any annuity contract would—nothing changes. Generally speaking, if you reach a point when you can't perform multiple functions of daily life on your own, you notify the

---

[12] A Place for Mom. January 2018. "Long-Term Care Insurance: Costs & Benefits." http://www.aplaceformom.com/senior-care-resources/articles/long-term-care-costs

insurance company, and a representative will turn on those provisions of your contract.

Like LTCI, different companies and products offer different options. Some annuity long-term care riders offer coverage of two years in a nursing home situation. Others cap expenses at two times the original annuity's value. It greatly depends. Some people prefer this option because there isn't a "use-it-or-lose-it" piece; if you die without ever having needed long-term care, you still will have had the income benefit from the base contract. However, as with any annuities or insurance contracts, there are the usual restrictions and limitations. Withdrawing money from the contract will affect future income payments, early distributions can result in a penalty, income taxes may apply, and, because the insurance company's solvency is what guarantees your payments, it's important to do your research about the insurance company you are considering purchasing a contract from.

Understandably, a discussion on long-term care is bound to feel at least a little tedious. Yet, this is a critical piece of planning for income in retirement, particularly if you want to leave a legacy.

As a Certified Elder Law Attorney (CELA®), I frequently receive calls from adult children whose parents have experienced some type of medical event like a stroke. The parents have no long-term care plan and face exorbitant monthly bills that could drain their life savings.

The earlier you start thinking about long-term care, the more options you'll have. One potential problem, however, could surface when paying for a long-term policy too early in life. The funds used might be better spent in an investment plan with the potential for better growth.

Spousal Planning

Here's one thing to keep in mind no matter how you plan to save: Many of us will be planning for more than ourselves. Look back at all the stats on health events and the likelihood of long life and long-term care. If they hold true for a single individual, then the likelihood of having a costly health or long-term care event is even higher for a married couple. You'll be planning for not just one life, but two. So, when it comes to long-term care insurance, annuities, self-funding, or whatever strategy you are looking at using, be sure you are funding longevity for the both of you.

Suppose a husband who handled most, if not all, financial obligations becomes afflicted by a devastating disease such as Alzheimer's. In that case, the difficulties faced by his wife could intensify if she faces any financial tumult.

To guard against such strain, it's possible to structure a holistic, long-term care plan capable of keeping an afflicted spouse comfortable for a period that allows the Medicaid five-year clock to continue running, so their assets are protected. Such a long-term plan can potentially reduce the cost of a nursing facility once that level of care becomes necessary.

Chapter 1: Longevity
KEY CONCEPTS

✓ In retirement, our resources are finite, but our lifespans can be unpredictably long

✓ Greater longevity can lead to additional costs stemming from health care and long-term care

✓ Planning for married couples should incorporate strategies designed to fund the longevity of each spouse

Look Ahead. . .Chapter 2: Taxes
What costs could arise from bearing the responsibility for federal resources we share?

CHAPTER 2

Taxes

*"What is the difference between a taxidermist and a tax
collector? The taxidermist takes only your skin."*
— *Mark Twain*

Where to begin with taxes? Perhaps by acknowledging we all bear responsibility for the resources we share. Roads, bridges, schools . . . It is the patriotic duty of every American to pay their fair share of taxes. Many would agree with me, though, while they don't mind paying their fair share, they're not interested in paying one cent more than that!

Now, just talking taxes probably takes your mind to April—tax season. You are probably thinking about all the forms you collect and how you file. Perhaps you are thinking about your certified public accountant or another qualified tax professional and saying to yourself, "I've already got taxes taken care of, thanks!"

However, what I see when people come into my office is that their relationship with their tax professional is purely a January through April relationship. That means they may have a tax professional, but not a tax *planner*.

What I mean is tax planning extends beyond filing taxes. In April, we are required to settle our accounts with the IRS to make sure we have paid up on our bill or to even the score if we have overpaid. But real tax planning is about making each

19

financial move in a way that allows you to keep the most money in your pocket and out of Uncle Sam's.

Now, as a caveat, I want to emphasize I am not a CPA, but I see the way taxes affect my clients, and I have plenty of experience helping clients implement tax-efficient strategies in their retirement plans in conjunction with their tax professionals. Additionally, our clients work with a CPA who is closely affiliated with our firm.

Many tax professionals or CPAs look through a micro lens of trying to minimize the taxes you pay in any specific year. We look at taxes through a macro lens, in order to help minimize the taxes you'll pay over your lifetime and maximize what you'll leave as a legacy.

In addition to tax planning with our affiliated CPA, we do tax preparation for our clients as part of our comprehensive Retirement and Legacy Blueprint Process.

It is especially important to me to help my clients develop tax-efficient strategies in their retirement plans because each dollar they can keep in their pockets is a dollar we can put to work.

Without getting political, I feel that I'm better at deciding how my money should be spent than the government. I am passionate about maintaining this kind of autonomy for myself and my clients.

One of the most important keys for making your retirement nest egg last as long as possible is understanding the different tax buckets that assets fall into and how each bucket affects you.

Understand the Tax Buckets

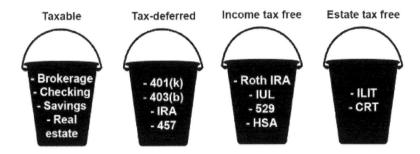

There are three main tax buckets (and a fourth to worry about depending on your net worth at death).

The first tax bucket is the taxable or post-tax bucket. This is composed of accounts and assets that you have already paid tax on, but now are taxed on the growth or gains. With these accounts, you receive a "love letter" from the IRS in the form of a 1099. This would be your checking, savings, money market, and brokerage accounts. What's important to know is that you may be taxed on capital gains from these accounts.

The second tax bucket to understand is the tax deferred bucket. With these accounts, when you pull any money out you are taxed at ordinary income tax rates. Accounts that fall into the tax deferred bucket are traditional 401(k)s, IRAs, 403(b)s, and 457s. These accounts you have not been taxed on yet. When you pull the money out, that is when you are taxed. If you take withdrawals before age fifty-nine-and-one-half, you may pay an additional 10% federal penalty, too.

The third tax bucket is most people's favorite and that is the tax-free bucket. These accounts can grow tax free. The big one that most people know about is the Roth IRA and also Roth 401ks, offered by employers, in which withdrawals are tax free after age fifty-nine-and-one-half and the account has been open for at least five years. Then there is Index Universal Life

Insurance (IULs). With an IUL, you can take a tax-free loan from your policy's cash values (if you have built up enough), and it will be deducted from your death benefit if you don't pay it back before you die. You need to manage your IUL policy carefully to ensure it doesn't lapse or require additional premiums to remain in force. In addition, the tax-free bucket includes 529s, which have to be used for educational funding, and HSAs, which have to be used to pay for health care.

Many of our clients want to move as much as they can to the tax-free bucket, given concerns about where taxes may be headed in the future.

The fourth tax bucket is what I call the tax-free plus bucket. The reason it is tax-free plus is because it is not subject to estate tax. There is a common misconception that the Roth IRA is completely tax-free. It is not. It is income tax-free, but it still is factored into the estate tax equation. An example of something that is estate tax free would be an IUL that has been moved into an Irrevocable Life Insurance Trust (ILIT). When your estate is larger than the estate tax exemption, then you need to consider not just the tax-free bucket, but the tax-free plus bucket. A Charitable Remainder Trust (CRT) lets you convert a highly appreciated asset, such as stocks or real estate, into lifetime income. It can reduce your income taxes while living and estate taxes following your death.

The Fed

Taxes in the United States can be a rather uncertain proposition. Depending on who is in the White House and which party controls Congress, we might be tempted to assume tax rates could either decline or increase in the next four to eight years accordingly. However, there is one (large!) factor we, as a nation, must confront: the national debt.

Currently, according to USDebtClock.org, we are over $26,500,000,000,000 in debt and climbing. That's $26.5 *trillion* with a "T." With just $1 trillion, you could park it in the bank at a zero percent interest rate and spend more than $54 million every day for fifty years without hitting a zero balance.

Even if Congress got a handle and stopped that debt from its daily compound, divided by each taxpayer, we each would owe about $214,000. So, will that be check or cash?

My point here isn't to give you anxiety. I'm just saying, even with the rosiest of outlooks on our personal income tax rates, none of us should count on low tax rates for the long term. Instead, you and your network of professionals (tax, legal, and financial) should constantly be looking for ways to take advantage of tax-saving opportunities as they come. After all, the best "luck" is when proper planning meets opportunity.

So, how can we get started?

Know Your Limits

One of the foundational pieces of tax planning is knowing what tax bracket you are in, based on your income after subtracting pre-tax or untaxed assets. Your income taxes are based on your taxable income.

One reason to know your taxable income and your income tax rate is so you can see how far away you are from the next lower or higher tax bracket. This is particularly important when it comes to decisions such as gifting and Roth IRA rollovers.

For instance, based on the 2022 tax table, Mallory and Ralph's taxable income is just over $345,000, putting them in the 32 percent tax bracket and about $4,900 above the upper end of the 24 percent tax bracket. They have already maxed out their retirement funds' tax-exempt contributions for the year. Their daughter, Gloria, is a sophomore in college. This couple could shave a considerable amount off their tax bill if they use the $4,900 to help Gloria out with groceries and school— something they were likely to do, anyway, but now can deliberately be put to work for them in their overall financial strategy.

Now, I use Mallory and Ralph only as an example—your circumstances are probably different—but I think this nicely illustrates the way planning ahead for taxes can save you money.

Assuming a Lower Tax Rate

Many people anticipate being in a lower tax bracket in retirement. It makes sense: You won't be contributing to retirement funds; you'll be drawing from them. And you won't have all those work expenses—work clothes, transportation, lunch meetings, etc.

Yet do you really plan on changing your lifestyle after retirement? Do you plan to cut down on the number of times you eat out, scale back vacations, and skimp on travel?

What I see in my office is many couples spend more in the first few years, or maybe the first decade, of retirement. Sure, that may taper off later on, but usually only just in time for their budget to be hit with greater health and long-term care expenses. Do you see where this is going? Many people plan as though their taxable income will be lower in retirement and are surprised when the tax bills come in and look more or less the same as they used to. It's better to plan for the worst and hope for the best, wouldn't you agree?

401(k)/IRA

One sometimes unexpected piece of tax planning in retirement concerns your 401(k) or IRA. Most of us have one of these accounts or an equivalent. Throughout our working lives, we pay in, dutifully socking away a portion of our earnings in these tax-deferred accounts. There's the rub: tax-deferred. Not tax-free. Very rarely is anything free of taxation when you get down to it. Using 401(k)s and IRAs in retirement is no different. The taxes the government deferred when you were in your working years are now coming due, and you will pay taxes on that income at whatever your current tax rate is.

Just to ensure Uncle Sam gets his due, the government also has a required minimum distribution, or RMD, rule. Beginning at age seventy-two, you are required to withdraw a certain minimum amount every year from your 401(k) or IRA, or else you will face a 50 percent tax penalty on any RMD monies you should have withdrawn but didn't—and that's on top of income tax.

Of course, there is also the Roth account. You can think of the difference between a Roth and a traditional retirement account as the difference between taxing the seed and taxing the harvest. Because Roths are funded with post-tax dollars, there aren't tax penalties for early withdrawals of the principal nor are there taxes on the growth after you reach age fifty-nine-and-one-half. Perhaps best of all, there are no RMDs. Of course, you must own a Roth account for a minimum of five years before you are able to take advantage of all its features.

This is one more area where it pays to be aware of your tax bracket. Some people may find it advantageous to "convert" their traditional retirement account funds to Roth account funds in a year during which they are in a lower tax bracket. Others may opt to put any excess RMDs from their traditional retirement accounts into other products, like stocks or insurance.

Does that make your head spin? Understandable. That's why it's so important to work with a financial professional and tax planner who can help you not only execute these sorts of tax-efficient strategies but also help you understand what you are doing and why.

Many of the clients I've worked with over the years came to me with virtually no tax strategy, but once we develop one, it can produce a significant net positive in their overall plan. Increasing one's wealth is often associated with wise investments. More often, however, wealth increases by lowering one's financial obligations.

When we develop a Retirement Tax Blueprint, we map out the year-by-year steps needed to help manage the effects of taxes throughout your retirement and for the legacy you leave.

I have noticed that couples who begin to really focus in on retirement in their late fifties have sometimes subscribed to an old adage. They "defer, defer, defer," meaning they place a majority of their savings into the tax-deferred bucket through plans offered by their employers, such as 401(k)s.

Different tax planning strategies we outline in our Retirement & Legacy Blueprint™ process can prove important when re-allocating savings accumulated in tax-deferred buckets.

Instead of overfunding the traditional 401(k), avenues can be explored to fortify the tax-free bucket with a Roth 401(k) or Index Universal Life Insurance. Such strategies can be mapped out to help diffuse the "ticking time bomb" that could affect existing 401(k)s during retirement. Strategic Roth conversions move money out of the tax-deferred bucket to get more into the tax-free bucket. Taxes will be assessed on the front end of such conversions, but that outlay can potentially be less than taxes people face in the future.

Chapter 2: Taxes
KEY CONCEPTS

✓ Tax planning goes beyond tax filing and incorporates strategies to help retain your hard-earned money

✓ Understanding your taxable income and your income tax rate can be vital when making some financial decisions

✓ Retirement may not reduce your taxable income.

Look Ahead. . .Chapter 3: Market Volatility
Can a balance be achieved between the needs to protect and grow your funds in retirement?

CHAPTER 3

Market Volatility

"Rule No.1: Never lose money.
"Rule No.2: Never forget rule No.1."
— *Warren Buffet*

U p and down. Roller coaster. Merry-go-round. Bulls and bears. Peak-to-trough.

Sound familiar? This is the language we use to talk about the stock market. With volatility and spikes, even our language is jarring, bracing, and vivid.

Still, financial strategies tend to revolve around market-based products, for good reasons. For one thing, there is no other financial class that packs the same potential for growth, pound for pound, as stock-based products. Because of growth potential, inflation protection, and new opportunities, it may be unwise to avoid the market entirely.

However, along with the potential for growth is the potential for loss. Many of the people I see in my office come in still feeling a bit burned from the market drama of 2000 to 2010. That was a rough stretch, and many of us are once-bitten-twice-shy investors, right?

So how do we balance these factors? How do we try to satisfy both the need for protection and the need for growth?

For one thing, it is important to recognize the value of diversity. Now, I'm not just talking about the diversity of assets among different kinds of stocks, or even different kinds of stocks and bonds. That's only one kind of diversity; while

29

important, both stocks and bonds, though different, are both still market-based products. Most market-based products, even within a diverse portfolio, tend to rise or lower as a whole, just like an incoming tide. Therefore, a portfolio diverse in only market-sourced products won't automatically protect your assets during times when the market declines.

In addition to the sort of "horizontal diversity" you have by purchasing a variety of stocks and bonds from different companies, I encourage having "vertical diversity," or diversity among asset classes. This means having different product types, including securities products, bank products, and insurance products—with varying levels of growth potential, liquidity, and protection—all in accordance with your unique situation, goals, and needs.

When we begin working with clients, we want them to gain a foundational understanding of two things: what investment tools are available and how most investments exist with only two of three distinctive characteristics.

Those would be protection, growth, and liquidity.

From there, we utilize a questionnaire that determines how much risk a client is willing to live with in retirement.

There are prudent guidelines to follow for managing risk levels in the market. Each guideline is based on a client's age. For example, the **"Rule of 100"** uses the following formula:

A hundred years old minus your actual age = maximum percentage of risk allocation.

So, a fifty-eight-year-old person would have a maximum risk allocation of 42 percent (100 − 58 = 42 percent).

The "Rule of 100" is a useful tool for making a quick assessment. Still, a thorough analysis usually requires sophisticated planning software capable of balancing risk and reward while incorporating a client's individual circumstances. The technology identifies risk factors in their existing portfolio and ultimately produces a "risk score," helping us better identify the investment tools to use. Each portfolio we structure at Castle Wealth Group is customized to meet your family's particular goals.

The Color of Money

When you're looking at the overall diversity of your portfolio, part of the equation is knowing which products fit in what category: what has liquidity, what has protection, and what has growth potential.

Before we dive in, keep in mind these aren't absolutes. You might think of liquidity, growth, and protection as primary colors. While some products will look pretty much yellow, red, or blue, others will have a mix of characteristics, making them more green, orange, or purple.

Growth

I like to think of the growth category as red. It's powerful, it's somewhat volatile, and it's also the category where we have the greatest opportunities for growth and loss. Often, products in the growth category will have a good deal of liquidity but very little protection. These are our market-based products and strategies, and we think of them mostly in shades of red and orange, to designate their growth and liquidity. This is a good place to be when you're young—think fast cars and flashy leather jackets—but its allure often wanes as you move closer to retirement. Examples of "red" products include:

- Stocks
- Equities
- Exchange-traded funds
- Mutual funds
- Corporate bonds
- Real estate investment trusts
- Speculations
- Alternative investments

Liquidity

Yellow is my liquid category color. I typically recommend having at least enough yellow money to cover six months' to a year's worth of expenses in case of emergency. Yellow assets don't need a lot of growth potential; they just need to be readily available when we need them. The "yellow" category includes assets like:

- Cash
- Money market accounts

Protection

The color of protection, to me, is green. Tranquil, peaceful, sure, even if it lacks a certain amount of flash. This is the direction I like to see people generally move toward as they're nearing retirement. The red, flashy look of stock market returns and the risk of possible overnight losses is less attractive as we near retirement and look for more consistency and reliability. While this category doesn't come with a lot of liquidity, the products here are backed by an insurance company, a bank, or a government entity. "Green" products include things such as:

- Certificates of deposit (backed by banks)
- Government-based bonds (backed by the U.S. government)
- Life insurance (backed by insurance companies)
- Annuities (backed by insurance companies)

401(k)s

I want to take a second to specifically address a tool many retirees will be using to build their retirement income: the 401(k) and other retirement accounts. Any of these retirement accounts (IRAs, 401(k)s, 403(b)s, etc.) are basically "tax wrappers." What do I mean by that? Well, depending on your plan provider, a 401(k) could include target-date funds, passively managed products, stocks, bonds, mutual funds, or even variable, fixed, and fixed index annuities, all collected in one place and governed by rules (a.k.a. the "tax wrapper"). These rules govern how much money you can put inside the wrapper, how you can put it in, when you will have to pay taxes on it, and when you can take the money out. Inside the 401(k), each of the products inside the "tax wrapper" might have its own fees or commissions, in addition to the management fee you pay on the 401(k) itself.

Now, fees can be troublesome. You can't get something for nothing, and fees are how many financial companies and professionals make a living. Yet, it's important to recognize even a fee of a single percentage point is money out of your pocket—money that represents not just the one-time fee of today but also represents an opportunity cost. One study found a single percentage point fee could cost a millennial close to $600,000 over forty years of saving.[13] For someone closer to retirement, how much do you think fees may have cost over their lifetime?

Even for those close to retirement, it's important to look at management fees and assess if you think you're getting what you pay for. Over the course of ten years, those puppies can add up, and you may have decades ahead of you in which you will need to rely on your assets.

Dollar-Cost Averaging

With 401(k)s and other market-based retirement products, when you are investing for the long term, dollar-cost averaging is a concept that can work in your favor. When the market is trending up, if you are consistently paying in money, month

---

[13] Dayana Yochim and Jonathan Todd. NerdWallet. "How a 1% Fee Could Cost Millennials $590,000 in Retirement Savings." https://www.nerdwallet.com/blog/investing/millennial-retirement-fees-one-percent-half-million-savings-impact/

over month, great; your investments can grow, and you are adding to your assets. When the market takes a dip, no problem; your dollars buy more shares at a lower price. At some point, we hope the market will rebound, in which case your shares can grow and possibly be more valuable than they were before. This concept is what we call "dollar-cost averaging." While it can't ensure a profit or guarantee against losses, it's a time-tested strategy for investing in a volatile market.

However, when you are in retirement, this strategy may work against you. You may have heard of "reverse" dollar-cost averaging. Before, when the market lost ground, you were "bargain-shopping"; your dollars purchased more assets at a reduced price. When you are in retirement, you are no longer the purchaser; you are selling. So, in a down market, you have to sell more assets to make the same amount of money as what you made in a favorable market.

I've had lots of people step into my office to talk to me about this, emphasizing "my advisor says the market always bounces back, and I have to just hold on for the long term."

There's some basis for this thinking; thus far, the market has always rebounded to higher heights than before. But this is no guarantee, and the prospect of potentially higher returns in five years may not be very helpful in retirement if you are relying on the income from those returns to pay this month's electric bill, for example.

As people move closer to retirement, one of the biggest concerns is "Sequence of Returns Risk." Meaning, that if the market declines now (like it did in 2008), given the amount of time before I retire, will it be enough to allow the market to recover? Many families lean more toward conservative investments as they near retirement as a way to move from the accumulation stage of life to the preservation and distribution stage.

The Retirement & Legacy Blueprint™ Process helps families identify an investment plan with reasonable fees and downside protections geared for their preferred risk tolerance.

Is There a "Perfect" Tool?

To bring us back around to the discussion of protection, growth, and liquidity, the ideal product would be a "ten" in all three categories, right? Completely guaranteed, doubling in size every few years, and accessible whenever you want. Does such a tool exist? No.

Instead of running in circles looking for that perfect tool, the silver bullet, the unicorn of financial strategies, it's more important to circle back to the concept of a balanced, asset-diverse portfolio.

This is why your interests may be best served when you work with a trusted financial professional who knows what various financial tools can do and how to use them in your personal retirement plan.

As a fiduciary and a financial advisor, I work to minimize the type of funds with higher cost transaction fees—the type sold by traditional brokers and dealers.

By lowering costs and fees, you can reduce financial obligations that can be especially burdensome in retirement—a point addressed in the next chapter.

Goal → Strategy → Tool

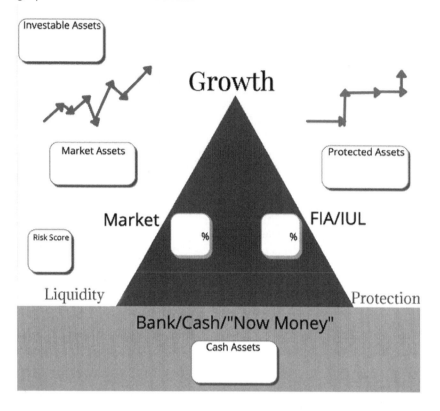

The graphic above shows how a portfolio can be allocated between the liquid money at the bank, the growth/liquid money in the market, and the growth money that is protected from market downturns but still can benefit from market growth.

The money in the market can be assigned a risk score of aggressive, moderate, or conservative.

Chapter 3: Market Volatility
KEY CONCEPTS

✓   Assessing management fees is always a sound approach, especially when relying on your assets in retirement

✓   In a down market during retirement, you must sell more assets to make the same amount of money as you previously did in a favorable market

✓   A balanced, asset-diverse portfolio can help satisfy the need for protection, growth, and liquidity

Look Ahead. . .Chapter 4: Retirement Income
How a financial professional can process a step-by-step plan and systematically build a balanced approach.

CHAPTER 4

Retirement Income

"There are few sorrows in which a good income is of no avail."
— *Logan Pearsall Smith*

Retirement. For many of us, it's what we've saved for and dreamed of, pinning our hopes to a magical someday. Is that someday full of traveling? Is it filled with grandkids? Gardening? Maybe your fondest dream is simply never having to work again, never having to clock in or be accountable to someone else.

Your ability to do these things all hinges on *income*. Without the money to support these dreams, even a basic level of work-free lifestyle is unsustainable. That's why planning for your income in retirement is so foundational. But where do we begin?

It's easy to feel overwhelmed by this question. Some may feel the urge to amass a large lump sum and then try to put it all in one product—insurance, investments, liquid assets—to provide all the growth, liquidity, and income they need. Instead, I think you need a more balanced approach. After all, retirement planning isn't magic. Like I mention elsewhere, there is no single product that can be all things to all people (or even all things to one person). No approach works unilaterally for everyone. That's why it's important to talk to a financial professional who can help you lay down the basics and take you step-by-step through the process. Not only will you have the assurance you have addressed the areas you need to, but you will also have an ally who can help you break down the process and help keep you from feeling overwhelmed.

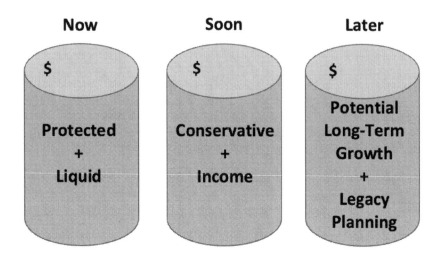

The above graphic shows how time horizons can be used to develop an income plan in financial planning.

The "Now" bucket is typically the money at the bank that covers your emergency fund, any big expenses coming up in the year and your income gap in retirement.

The "Later" bucket is money that is geared towards long-term growth, long-term care, and legacy.

The "Soon" bucket is your bridge of protected, conservative income to help bridge the "Now" and "Later" buckets.

The income plan can help drive the investment plan and tax plan because the different buckets should be invested differently based on time horizons.

Sources of Income

Thinking of all the pieces of your retirement expenses might be intimidating. But, like cleaning out a junk drawer or revisiting that garage remodel, once you have laid everything out, you can begin to sort things into categories.

Once you have a good overall picture of where your expenses will lie, you can start stacking up the resources to cover them.

Social Security

Social Security is a guaranteed, inflation-protected federal insurance program playing a significant part in most of our retirement plans. From delaying until you've reached full retirement age or beyond to examining spousal benefits, as I discuss elsewhere in this book, there is plenty you can do to try to make the most of this monthly benefit. As with all your retirement income sources, it's important to consider how to make this resource stretch to provide the most bang and buck for your situation.

Pension

Another generally reliable source of retirement income for you might be a pension, if you are one of the lucky people who still has one.

If you don't have a pension, go ahead and skim on to the next section. If you do have a pension, keep on reading.

Because your pension can be such a central piece of your retirement income plan, you will want to put some thought into answering basic questions about it.

How well is your pension funded? Since the heyday of the pension plan, companies and governments have neglected to fund their pension obligations, causing a persistent problem with this otherwise reliable asset. Public pensions face a collective $4.7 trillion deficit, according to the U.S. Pension Tracker.[14] The Public Benefit Guaranty Association, which helps ensure private pensions, reports there is a $54 billion shortfall in multiemployer plans, affecting half of all

---

[14] U.S. Pension Tracker. April 2019. us.pensiontracker.org

multiemployer plans.[15] If you have a pension, it is quite possibly included in those statistics.

In addition to checking up on your pension's health, check into what your options are for withdrawing your pension. If you have already retired and made those decisions, this may be a foregone conclusion. If not, it pays to know what you can expect and what decisions you can make, such as taking spousal options to cover your husband or wife if he or she outlives you.

Also, some companies are incentivizing lump-sum payouts of pensions to reduce the companies' payment liabilities. If that's the case with your employer, talk to your financial professional to see if it might be prudent to do something like that or if it might be better to stick with lifetime payments or other options.

Your 401(k) and IRA

One "modern way" to save for retirement is in a 401(k) or IRA (or their nonprofit or governmental equivalents). These tax-advantaged accounts are, in my opinion, a poor substitute for pensions, but one of the biggest disservices we do to ourselves is to not take full advantage of them in the first place. According to one article, about 42 percent of adults under thirty and 26 percent of adults thirty to forty-four haven't contributed to any retirement account, let alone their 401(k).[16]

Also, if you have changed jobs over the years, do the work of tracking down any benefits from your past employers. You might have an IRA here or a 401(k) there; keep track of

---

[15] Alessandro Malito. MarketWatch. December 11, 2018. "The Truth About Pensions: They Aren't Dead, But Some Are Barely Holding On." https://www.marketwatch.com/story/the-truth-about-pensions-they-arent-dead-but-some-are-barely-holding-on-2018-12-11

[16] Niall McCarthy. Forbes. June 3, 2019. "Report: A Quarter of Americans Have No Retirement Savings." https://www.forbes.com/sites/niallmccarthy/2019/06/03/report-a-quarter-of-americans-have-no-retirement-savings-infographic/#5fb35b703ebf

those so you can pull them together and look at those assets when you're ready to look at establishing sources of retirement income.

Do You Have...

- Life insurance?
- Annuities?
- Long-term care insurance?
- Any passive income sources?
- Stock and bond portfolios?
- Liquid assets? (What's in your bank account?)
- Alternative investments?
- Rental properties?

It's important, if you are going through the work of sitting with a financial professional, to look at your full retirement income picture and pull together *all* your assets, no matter how big or small. From the free insurance policy offered at your bank to the sizable investment in your brother-in-law's modestly successful furniture store, you want to have a good idea of where your money is.

I sat down with a retired couple recently. He'd been an engineer and she a nurse. During the accumulation phase of their lives, they had changed jobs several times and had multiple retirement accounts spread out in various places.

As we went through the Retirement & Legacy Blueprint™ Process, we built a list of their assets, and for the first time, they were able to see the sum of their efforts. They were astonished to learn that they had accumulated over $2 million in liquid assets.

They had initially come to us concerned about whether they would have enough to retire. We consolidated everything their sweat equity had produced and explained how their assets could be used to create a new kind of income in retirement. For many, delving into the question of whether their savings will last is the most stressful part of retiring. That stress often disappears once people learn what their savings can do for them. The information that comes from building a retirement plan can be illuminating because it identifies how various accounts will be set up for the future – a future that might last another thirty years or more.

Retirement Income Needs

How much income will you need in retirement? How do you determine that? A lot of people work toward a random number, thinking, "If I can just have a million dollars, I'll be comfortable in retirement!" Don't get me wrong; it is possible to save up a lot of money and then retire in the hopes you can keep your monthly expenses lower than some set estimation. But I think this carries a general risk of running out of money. Instead, I work with my clients to find out what their current and projected income needs are and then work from there to see how we might cover any gaps between what they have and what they want.

Goals and Dreams

I like to start with your pie in the sky. Do you find yourself planning for your vacations more thoroughly than you do your retirement? A recent survey found one in five Americans spends more time planning our vacations than we spend planning our retirements.[17] Maybe it's because planning a vacation is less stressful: Having a week at the beach go awry is, well, a walk on the beach compared to running out of money in retirement. Whatever the case, perhaps it would be better if you thought of your retirement as a vacation in and of itself—no

---

[17] Malika Mitra. CNBC. August 2, 2019. "You're not alone if you spend more time planning your vacation than working on your finances." https://www.cnbc.com/2019/08/02/1-in-5-people-spend-more-time-planning-vacations-than-finances-survey.html

clocking in, no boss, no overtime. If you felt unlimited by financial strain, what would you do?

Would an endless vacation for you mean Paris and Rome? Would it mean mentoring at children's clubs or serving at the local soup kitchen? Or maybe it would mean deepening your ties to those immediately around you—neighbors, friends, and family. Maybe it would mean more time to take part in the hobbies and activities you love. Have you been considering a second (or even third) act as a small-business owner, turning a hobby or passion into a revenue source?

This is your time to daydream and answer the question: If you could do anything, what would you do?

After that, it's a matter of putting a dollar amount on it. What are the costs of round-the-world travel? One couple I know said their highest priority in retirement was being able to take each of their grandchildren on a cross-country vacation every year. That's a pretty specific goal—one that is reasonably easy to nail down a budget for.

Every family's goals for retirement are different. One concept I stress to clients, regardless of their stage of life, is to always have something to look forward to. This advice does not change for someone in retirement. Too often, people retire without a plan for what's next. So it helps to ask what will keep me engaged, happy, and active?

I have some clients whose goal is to be able to stay at home and work on projects in the garage or garden. I have other clients who love traveling the world and going on cruises. Retirement is not a one-size-fits-all proposition like many of the "Big Box" investment firms make it seem. Each time we sit down with a family, we walk through a detailed goal analysis as part of the Retirement & Legacy Blueprint™ Process. We design this analysis to help make sure your retirement fits you.

Current Budget

Compiling a current expense report is one of the trickiest pieces of retirement preparation. Many people assume the expenses of their lives in retirement will be different—lower. After all, there will be no drive to work, no need for a formal wardrobe, and, perhaps most impactful of all, no more saving for retirement!

It is very important to calculate what we call the "income gap." First, we must calculate the monthly amount derived from fixed income sources like pensions (for those fortunate enough to still have them) and Social Security. Second, we must determine the sum of basic monthly expenses anticipated in retirement. Once we learn the difference between these two calculations, we can use that amount to begin developing an income plan.

Many of our families need 80 to 100 percent of the income they required while working to cover all of their expenses in retirement. Some could even need more income depending on their goals. I believe the best method for estimating expenses is to go through at least a few months of bank statements. This exercise provides a clear understanding of spending, which may or may not include purchases outside your normal bills (utilities, taxes, mortgage, food, car loans).

I can't count the number of times I have sat with a couple, asked them about their spending, and heard them throw out a number that seemed incredibly low. When I ask them where the number came from, they usually say they estimated based on their total bills. Yet, our spending is so much more than our mortgage, utilities, cable, phone, car, grocery, or credit card bills.

"What about clothes?" I ask, "Or dining out? What about gifts and coffees and last-minute birthday cards?" That's when the lights come on.

This is why I suggest actually collecting a year's worth of information. There is usually no such thing as a one-time purchase. Did you buy new furniture? Even if that is a rarity, do you think that will be the last time you *ever* buy furniture?

Another hefty expense is spending on the kids. Many of the couples I work with are quick to help their adult children, whether it's something like letting them live in the basement, paying for college, babysitting, paying an occasional bill, or contributing to a grandchild's college fund. They aren't alone— 79 percent of Americans in 2018 said they had provided financial support for an adult child. And it's not unlikely for some parents to tap into their retirement funds to do so.[18]

My clients sometimes protest that what they do for their grown children can stop in retirement. They don't *need* to help. But I get it. Parents like to feel needed. And, while you never want to neglect saving for retirement in favor of taking on financial risks (like your child's student debt), the parents who help their adult children do so in part because it helps them feel fulfilled.

When it comes down to expenses, including (and especially) spending on your family, don't make your initial calculations based on what you *could* whittle your budget down to if you *had* to. Instead, start from where you are. Who wants to live off a bare-bones bank account in retirement?

Other Expenses

Once you have nailed down your current budget and your dreams or goals for retirement, there are a few other outstanding pieces to think about—some expenses many people don't take the time to consider before making and executing a plan. But I'm assuming you want to get it right, so let's take a look.

Housing

Do you know where you want to live in retirement? This makes up a substantial piece of your income puzzle—since the typical

---

[18] Lorie Konish. CNBC. October 2, 2018. "Parents Spend Twice as Much on Adult Children than They Save for Retirement."
https://www.cnbc.com/2018/10/02/parents-spend-twice-as-much-on-adult-children-than-saving-for-retirement.html

American household owns a home, and it's generally their largest asset.

Some people prefer to live right where they are for as long as they can. Others have been waiting for retirement to pull the trigger on an ambitious move, like purchasing a new house, or even downsizing. Whatever your plans and whatever your reasons, there are quite a few things to consider.

Mortgage

Do you still have a mortgage? What may have been a nice tax boon in your working years could turn into a financial burden in your retirement. After all, when you are on a limited income, a mortgage is just one more bill sapping your financial strength. It is something to put some thought into, whether you plan to age in place or are considering moving to your dream home, buying a house out of state, or living in a retirement community.

Upkeep and Taxes

A house without a mortgage still requires annual taxes. While it's tempting to think of this as a once-a-year expense, when you have limited earning potential, your annual tax bill might be something into which you should put a little more forethought.

The costs of homeownership aren't just monetary. When you find yourself dealing with more house than you need, it can drain your time and energy. From keeping clutter at bay to keeping the lawn mower running, upkeep can be extensive and expensive. For some, that's a challenge they heartily accept and can comfortably take on. For others, the idea of yard work or cleaning an area larger than they need feels foolish.

For instance, Peggy discovered after her knee replacement that most of her house was inaccessible to her when she was laid up.

"It felt ridiculous to pay someone else to dust and vacuum a house I was only living in 40 percent of!"

Practicality and Adaptability

Erik and Magda are looking to retire within the next two decades. They just sold their old three-bedroom ranch-style house. Their twins are in high school, and the couple has wanted to "upgrade" for years. Now they live in a gorgeous 1940s three-story house with all the kitchen space they ever wanted, five sprawling bedrooms, and a library and media room for themselves and their children. Within months of moving in, the couple realized a house perfect for their active teens would no longer be perfect for them in five to fifteen years.

"We are paying the mortgage for this house, but we've started saving for the next one," said Magda, "because who wants to climb two flights of stairs to their bedroom when they're seventy-eight?"

Others I know have encountered a similar situation in their personal lives. After a health crisis, one couple found the luxurious tub for two they toiled to install had become a specter of a bad slip and a potential safety risk. It's important to think through what your physical reality could be. I always emphasize to my clients that they should plan for whatever their long-term future might hold, but it's amazing how many people don't give it much thought.

Contracts and Regulations

If you are looking into a cross-country move, be aware of new tax tables or local ordinances in the area where you are looking to move. After all, you don't want to experience sticker-shock when you are looking at downsizing or reducing your bills in retirement.

Along the same lines, if you are moving into a retirement community, be sure to look at the fine print. What happens if you must move into a different situation for long-term care? Will you be penalized? Will you be responsible for replacing your slot in the community? What are all the fees, and what do they cover?

Inflation

As I write this in 2022, America has experienced a wave of inflation following a lengthy period of low inflation. Inflation zoomed to 6.8% in November 2021, its highest mark since June 1982.[19]

Core inflation is yet another measurement that excludes goods with prices that tend to be more volatile, such as food and energy costs. Core inflation for a 12-month period ending in November 2021 was 4.9 percent. It so happened energy prices rose a whopping 33.3 percent over that timeframe.[20]

However, inflation isn't a one-time bump; it has a cumulative effect. Again, that can impact the price of groceries greater than other goods. Even with relatively low inflation over the past few decades, the jar of peanut butter you bought in 1997 for $2.48 will cost $4.18 today. A $100 ticket to a 1997 sporting event now costs $221.11.[21] Some of you might choose to watch from home and eat a peanut butter sandwich.

What if, in retirement, we hit a stretch like the late seventies and early eighties, when annual inflation rates of 10 percent became the norm? It may be wise to consider some extra padding in your retirement income plan to account for any potential increase in inflation in the future.

Aging

Also, in the expense category, think about longevity. We all hope to age gracefully. However, it's important to face the prospect of aging with a sense of realism.

---

[19] tradingeconomics.com. 2022 Data/2023 Forecast/1914-2021 Historical. "United States Inflation Rate" https://tradingeconomics.com/united-states/inflation-cpi

[20] U.S. Inflation Calculator. "United States Core Inflation Rates (1957-2021)" https://www.usinflationcalculator.com/inflation/united-states-core-inflation-rates/

[21] Ibid.

The elephant in the room for many families is long-term care: No one wants to admit they will likely need it, but estimates say as many as 70 percent of us will. [22] Aging is a significant piece of retirement income planning because you'll want to figure out how to set aside money for your care, either at home or away from it. The more comfortable you get with discussing your wishes and plans with your loved ones, the easier planning for the financial side of it can be.

I discuss health care and potential long-term care costs in more detail elsewhere in this book, but suffice it to say nursing home care tends to be very expensive and typically isn't something you get to choose when you will need.

It isn't just the costs of long-term care that pose a concern in living longer. It's also about covering the possible costs of everything else associated with living longer. For instance, if Henry retires from his job as a biochemical engineer at age sixty-five, perhaps he planned to have a very decent income for twenty years, until age eighty-five. But what if he lives until he's ninety-five? That's a whole third—ten years—more of personal income he will need.

Putting It All Together

Whew! So, you have pulled together what you have, and you have a pretty good idea of where you want to be. Now your financial professional, legal professional, and you can go about the work of arranging what assets you *have* to cover what you *need*—and how you might try to cover any gaps.

Like the proverbial man in the Bible who built his house on a rock, I like to help my clients figure out how to cover their day-to-day living expenses—their needs—with insurance and other guaranteed income sources like pensions and Social Security.

---

[22] Moll Law Group. 2021. "The Cost of Long-Term Care." https://www.molllawgroup.com/the-cost-of-long-term-care.html

With a Retirement & Legacy Blueprint™, income planning is the foundation of the fiscal house that everything else relies on for stability. Once retirement income is determined, you can begin planning your investments, taxes, health care, and legacy plan. Income planning is the first big step and it helps give families the clarity, confidence, and comfort they need to retire.

Again, you should keep in mind there isn't one single financial vehicle, asset, or source to fill all your needs, and that's okay. One of the challenges of planning for your income in retirement concerns figuring out what products and strategies to use. You can release some of that stress when you accept the fact you will probably need a diverse portfolio—potentially with bonds, stocks, insurance, and other income sources—not just one massive money pile.

One way to help shore up your income gaps is by working with your financial professional and a qualified tax advisor to mitigate your tax exposure. If you have a 401(k) or IRA, a tax advisor in your corner can help you figure out how and when to take distributions from your account in a way that doesn't push you into a higher tax bracket. Or you might learn how to use tax-advantaged bonds more effectively. Effective tax planning isn't necessarily about "adding" to your income. Especially regarding retirement, it's less about what you make than it is about what you keep. Paying a lower tax bill keeps more money in your pocket, which is where you want it when it comes to retirement income.

Now you can look at ways to cover your remaining retirement goals. Are there products like long-term care insurance specific to a certain kind of expense you anticipate? Is there a particular asset you want to use for your "play" money—money for trips and gifts for the grandkids? Is there any way you can portion off money for those charitable legacy plans?

Once you have analyzed your income wants, needs, and the assets to realistically cover them, you may have a gap. The masterstroke of a competent financial professional will be to help you figure out how you will cover that gap. Will you need to cut out a round of golf a week? Maybe skip the new car? Or will you need to take more substantial action?

One way to cover an income gap is to consider working longer or even part-time before retirement and even after that magical calendar date. This may not be the best "plan" for you; disabilities, work demands, and physical or emotional limitations can hinder the best-laid plans to continue working. However, if it is physically possible for you, this is one considerable way to help your assets last.

In fact, about one in five Americans are still working past age sixty-five. This is a record percentage in the past half-century. While some do list their personal finances as a reason for staying on the job, others do so to avoid feeling bored in retirement, among other reasons.[23]

Retirement is freedom—freedom to spend your time how you want, where you want, and with whom you want. Kind of different than having to be at the same place every day at 8 a.m. Most of all, retirement should be free of stress. When I help clients seeking the clarity and confidence to enjoy the rest of their years on their terms, I'm often told, "this feels like a gift." Of course, they did the hard part, but I'm thankful to hear it anyway.

Often, people come to us wanting to know the answer to one question as they near retirement: "Am I going to be okay?" Doubts they may have sometimes stem from uncertainty attempting to arrange all the components of their retirement puzzle. Seeing a comprehensive plan that addresses all potential issues can be comforting, beginning with a thorough analysis of their income needs moving forward.

I'm reminded of a client, we'll call him Cliff. Cliff was tired of driving into Dearborn every day, a point he emphasized as we chatted about how he wanted to retire.. After mapping out his Retirement & Legacy Blueprint™, Cliff's fervent hope would be

[23] Associated Press. October 9, 2018. "1 in 5 Americans over 65 are Still Waiting to Retire." https://nypost.com/2018/10/09/1-in-5-americans-over-65-are-still-waiting-to-retire/

to tell someone in human resources that he was one bad snowstorm from retirement. His commute was bad enough without having to worry about snowy conditions and the white-knuckle delays they could cause.

Cliff could detect options available to him simply by examining a thorough retirement income plan that outlined different variables that could arise once he left the workforce.

And yes, Cliff did retire one December after a bad snowstorm and hasn't looked back.

When you're retired, you no longer have an employer paying you a steady check. It is up to you to make sure you have saved and planned for the income you need.

Chapter 4: Retirement Income
KEY CONCEPTS

✓ No single financial product or approach can be all things to all people. A financial professional can help establish basic tenets and aid in building a process

✓ A financial professional can help you determine your current and projected income needs and how to cover potential gaps

✓ Inflation can have a cumulative effect you should account for in your retirement income plan

Look Ahead. . .Chapter 5: Social Security
Understanding various options can help you determine the best approach for taking your benefits.

Social Security

"(Social Security) represents our commitment as a society to the belief that workers should not live in dread that a disability, death, or old age could leave them or their families destitute."
—*Jimmy Carter*

Social Security is often the foundation of retirement income. Backed by the strength of the U.S. Treasury, it provides perhaps the most dependable paycheck you will have in retirement.

From the time you collect your first paycheck from the job that made you a bona fide taxpayer (for me, it was as a lifeguard at the Farmington Hills YMCA), you are paying into the grand old Social Security system. What grew and developed out of the pressures of the Great Depression has become one of the most popular government programs in the country, and, if you pay in for the equivalent of ten years or more, you, too, can benefit from the Social Security program.

Now, before we get into the nitty-gritty of Social Security, I'd like to address a current concern: Will Social Security still be there for you when you reach retirement age?

The Future of Social Security

This question is ever-present as headlines trumpet an underfunded Social Security program, alongside the sea of baby boomers who are retiring in droves and the comparatively smaller pool of younger people who are bearing the responsibility of funding the system.

The Social Security Administration itself acknowledges this concern as each Social Security statement now bears an asterisk that continues near the end of the summary:

> *"*Your estimated benefits are based on current law. Congress has made changes to the law in the past and can do so at any time. The law governing benefit amounts may change because, by 2034, the payroll taxes collected will be enough to pay only about 79 percent of scheduled benefits."*

Just a reminder, as if you needed one, that nothing in life is guaranteed. Additionally, depending on who you're listening to, Social Security funds may run low before 2034 thanks to the financial instability and government spending that accompanied the 2020 COVID-19 pandemic.

Before you get too discouraged, though, here are a few thoughts to keep you going:

- Even if the program is only paying 79 cents on the dollar for scheduled benefits, 79 percent is notably not zero.
- The Social Security Administration has made changes in the distant and near past to protect the fund's solvency, including increasing retirement ages and striking certain filing strategies.
- There are many changes Congress could make, and lawmakers are currently discussing how to fix the system, such as further increasing full retirement age and eligibility.
- One thing no one is seriously discussing? Reneging on current obligations to retirees or the soon-to-retire.

Take heart. The real answer to the question, "Will Social Security be there for me?" is still yes.

This question is an important one to consider when you look at how much we, as a nation, rely on this program. Did you know Social Security benefits replace about 40 percent of a person's original income when they retire?[24]

If you ask me, that's a pretty significant piece of your retirement income puzzle.

Another caveat? You may not realize this, but no one can legally "advise" you about your Social Security benefits.

"But, Chris," you may be thinking, "isn't that part of what you do? And what about that nice gentleman at the Social Security Administration office I spoke with on the phone?"

Don't get me wrong. Social Security Administration employees know their stuff. They are trained to know policies and programs, and they are usually pretty quick to tell you what you can and cannot do. But the government specifically says, because Social Security is a benefit you alone have paid into and earned, your Social Security decisions, too, are yours alone.

When it comes to financial professionals, we can't push you in any directions, either, *but*—there's a big "but" here—working with a well-informed financial professional is still incredibly handy when it comes to your Social Security decisions. Why? Because someone who's worth his or her salt will know what withdrawal strategies might pertain to your specific situation and will ask questions that can help you determine what you are looking for when it comes to your Social Security.

For instance, some people want the highest possible monthly benefit. Others want to start their benefits early, not always because of financial need. I heard about one man who called in to start his Social Security payments the day he qualified, just because he liked to think of it as the government paying back a debt it owed him, and he enjoyed the feeling of receiving a check from Uncle Sam.

Whatever your reasons, questions, or feelings regarding Social Security, the decision is yours alone; but working with a

---

[24] Social Security Administration. "Learn About Social Security Programs." https://www.ssa.gov/planners/retire/r&m6.html

financial professional can help you put your options in perspective by showing you—both with industry knowledge and with proprietary software or planning processes—where your benefits fit into your overall strategy for retirement income.

One reason the federal government doesn't allow for "advice" related to Social Security, I suspect, is so no one can profit from giving you advice related to your Social Security benefit—or from providing any clarifications. Again, this is a sign of a good financial professional. Those who are passionate about their work will be knowledgeable about what benefit strategies might be to your advantage and will happily share those possible options with you.

Full Retirement Age

When it comes to Social Security, it seems like many people only think so far as "yes." They don't take the time to understand the various options available. Instead, because it is common knowledge you can begin your benefits at age sixty-two, that's what many of us do. While more people are opting to delay taking benefits, age sixty-two is still firmly the most popular age to start.[25]

What many people fail to understand is, by starting benefits early, they may be leaving a lot of money on the table. You see, the Social Security Administration bases your monthly benefit on two factors: your earnings history and your full retirement age (FRA).

From your earnings history, they pull the thirty-five years you made the most money and use a mathematical indexing formula to figure out a monthly average from those years. If you paid into the system for less than thirty-five years, then every year you didn't pay in will be counted as a zero.

[25] Elizabeth O'Brien. Money. March 7, 2019. "This is the Age when Most People Claim Social Security—and When Experts Say You Really Should." http://money.com/money/5637694/this-is-the-age-when-most-people-claim-social-security-and-when-experts-say-you-really-should/

Once they have calculated what your monthly earning would be at FRA, the government then calculates what to put on your check based on how close you are to FRA. FRA was originally set at sixty-five, but, as the population aged and lifespans lengthened, the government shifted FRA later and later, based on an individual's year of birth. Check out the following chart to see when you will reach FRA. [26]

---

[26] Social Security Administration. "Full Retirement Age." https://www.ssa.gov/planners/retire/retirechart.html

Age to Receive Full Social Security Benefits*	
(Called "full retirement age" [FRA] or "normal retirement age.")	
Year of Birth*	FRA
1937 or earlier	65
1938	65 and 2 months
1939	65 and 4 months
1940	65 and 6 months
1941	65 and 8 months
1942	65 and 10 months
1943-1954	66
1955	66 and 2 months
1956	66 and 4 months
1957	66 and 6 months
1958	66 and 8 months
1959	66 and 10 months
1960 and later	67
*If you were born on Jan. 1 of any year, you should refer to the previous year. (If you were born on the 1st of the month, we figure your benefit [and your full retirement age] as if your birthday was in the previous month.)	

When you reach FRA, you are eligible to receive 100 percent of whatever the Social Security Administration says is your full monthly benefit.

Starting at age sixty-two, for every year before FRA you claim benefits, your monthly check is reduced by 5 percent or more. Conversely, for every year you delay taking benefits past FRA, your monthly benefit increases by 8 percent (until age seventy—after that, there is no monetary advantage to delaying Social Security benefits). While your circumstances and needs may vary, a lot of financial professionals still urge people to at least consider delaying until they reach age seventy.

Why wait?[27]

Taking benefits early could affect your monthly check by _____.								
62	63	64	65	FRA 66	67	68	69	70
-25%	-20%	-13.3%	-6.7%	0	+8%	+16%	+24%	+32%

My Social Security

If you are over age thirty, you have probably received a notice from the Social Security Administration telling you to activate something called "My Social Security." This is a handy way to learn more about your particular benefit options, to keep track of what your earnings record looks like, and to calculate the benefits you have accrued over the years.

Essentially, My Social Security is an online account you can activate to see what your personal Social Security picture looks like, which you can do at www.ssa.gov/myaccount. This can be extremely helpful when it comes to planning for income in retirement and figuring up the difference between your anticipated income versus anticipated expenses.

---

[27] Social Security Administration. April 2019. "Can You Take Your Benefits Before Full Retirement Age?"
https://www.ssa.gov/planners/retire/applying2.html

My Social Security is also helpful because it's a great way to see if there is a problem. For instance, I have heard of one woman who, through diligently checking her tax records against her Social Security profile, discovered her Social Security check was shortchanging her, based on her earnings history. After taking the discrepancy to the Social Security Administration, they sent her what they owed her in makeup benefits.

COLA

Social Security is a largely guaranteed piece of the retirement puzzle: If you get a statement that says to expect $1,000 a month, you can be sure you will receive $1,000 a month. But there is one variable detail, and that is something called the cost-of-living adjustment, or COLA.

The COLA is an increase in your monthly check meant to address inflation in everyday life. After all, your expenses will likely continue to experience inflation in retirement, but you will no longer have the opportunity for raises, bonuses, or promotions you had when you were working. Instead, Social Security receives an annual cost-of-living increase tied to the Department of Labor's Consumer Price Index for Urban Wage Earners and Clerical Workers, or CPI-W. If the CPI-W measurement shows inflation rose a certain amount for regular goods and services, then Social Security recipients will see that reflected in their COLA.

The COLA averages 4 percent, but in a no- or low-inflation environment, such as in 2010, 2011, and 2016, Social Security recipients will not receive an adjustment. Some view the COLA as a perk, bump, or bonus, but, in reality, it works more like this: Your mom sends you to the store with $2.50 for a gallon of milk. Milk costs exactly $2.50. The next week, you go back with that same amount, but it is now $2.52 for a gallon, so you go back to Mom, and she gives you 2 cents. You aren't bringing home more milk—it just costs more money.

So the COLA is less about "making more money" and more about keeping seniors' purchasing power from eroding when inflation is a big factor, such as in 1975, when it was 8 percent![28] Still, don't let that detract from your enthusiasm about COLAs; after all, what if Mom's solution was: "Here's the same $2.50; try to find pennies from somewhere else to get that milk!"?

Spousal Benefits

We've talked about FRA, but another big Social Security decision involves spousal benefits.

If you or your spouse has a long stretch of zeros in your earnings history—perhaps if one of you stayed home for years, caring for children or sick relatives—you may want to consider filing for spousal benefits instead of filing on your own earnings history. A spousal benefit can be up to 50 percent of the primary wage earner's benefit at full retirement age.

To begin drawing a spousal benefit, you must be at least sixty-two years old, and the primary wage earner must have already filed for his or her benefit. While there are penalties for taking spousal benefits early (you could lose up to 67.5 percent of your check for filing at age sixty-two), you cannot earn credits for delaying past full retirement age.[29]

Like I said, the spousal benefit can be a big deal for those who don't have a very long pay history, but it's important to weigh your own earned benefits against the option of withdrawing based on a fraction of your spouse's benefits.

To look at how this could play out, let's use a hypothetical couple: Mary Jane, who is sixty, and Peter, who is sixty-two.

Let's say Peter's benefit at FRA, in his case sixty-six, would be $1,600. If Peter begins his benefits right now, four years before FRA, his monthly check will be $1,200. If Mary Jane

---

[28] Social Security Administration. "Cost-Of-Living Adjustment (COLA) Information for 2019." https://www.ssa.gov/cola/.

[29] Social Security Administration. "Retirement Planner: Benefits For You As A Spouse." https://www.ssa.gov/planners/retire/applying6.html

begins taking spousal benefits in two years at the earliest date possible, her monthly benefits will be reduced by 67.5 percent, to $520 per month (remember, at FRA, the most she can qualify for is half of Peter's FRA benefit).

What if Peter and Mary Jane both wait until FRA? At sixty-six, Peter begins taking his full benefit of $1,600 a month. Two years later, when she reaches age sixty-six, Mary Jane will qualify for $800 a month. By waiting until FRA, the couple's monthly benefit goes from $1,720 to $2,400.

What if Peter delays until age seventy to get his maximum possible benefit? For each year past FRA he delays, his monthly benefits increase by 8 percent. This means, at seventy, he could file for a monthly benefit of $2,112. However, delayed retirement credits do not affect spousal benefits, so as soon as Peter files at seventy, Mary Jane would also file (at age sixty-eight) for her maximum benefit of $800, so their highest possible combined monthly check is $2,912.[30]

When it comes to your Social Security benefits, you obviously will want to consider whether a monthly check based on a fraction of your spouse's earnings will be comparable to or larger than your own earnings history.

Divorced Spouses

There are a few considerations for those of us who have gone through a divorce. If you 1) were married for ten years or more *and* 2) have since been divorced for at least two years *and* 3) are unmarried *and* 4) your ex-spouse qualifies to begin Social Security, you qualify for a spousal benefit based on your ex-husband or ex-wife's earnings history at FRA. A divorced spousal benefit is different from the married spousal benefit in

---

[30] Office of the Chief Actuary. Social Security Administration. "Social Security Benefits: Benefits for Spouses." https://www.ssa.gov/OACT/quickcalc/spouse.html#calculator

one way: You don't have to wait for your ex-spouse to file before you can file yourself.[31]

For instance, Charles and Moira were married for fifteen years before their divorce, when he was thirty-six and she was forty. Moira has been remarried for twenty years, and, although Charles briefly remarried, his second marriage ended after a few years. Charles' benefits are largely calculated based on his many years of volunteering in schools, meaning his personal monthly benefit is close to zero.

Although Moira has deferred her retirement, opting to delay benefits until she is seventy, Charles can begin taking benefits calculated from Moira's work history at FRA as early as sixty-two. However, he will also have the option of waiting until FRA to collect the maximum, or 50 percent of Moira's earned monthly benefit at her FRA.

Widowed Spouses

If your marriage ended with the death of your spouse, you might claim a benefit for your spouse's earned income as his or her widow/widower, called a survivor's benefit. Unlike a spousal benefit or divorced benefits, if your husband or wife dies, you can claim his or her full benefit. Also, unlike spousal benefits, if you need to, you can begin taking income when you turn sixty. However, as with other benefit options, your monthly check will be permanently reduced for withdrawing benefits before FRA.

If your spouse began taking benefits before he or she died, you can't delay withdrawing your survivor's benefits to get delayed credits; the Social Security Administration says you can

---

[31] Social Security Administration. "Retirement Planner: If You Are Divorced." https://www.ssa.gov/planners/retire/divspouse.html

only get as much from a survivor's benefit as your deceased spouse might have gotten, had he or she lived.[32]

Taxes, Taxes, Taxes

With Social Security, as with everything, it is important to consider taxes. It may be surprising, but your Social Security benefits are not tax-free. Despite having been taxed to accrue those benefits in the first place, you may have to pay Uncle Sam income taxes on up to 85 percent of your Social Security.

The Social Security Administration figures these taxes using what they call "the provisional income formula." Your provisional income formula differs from the adjusted gross income you use for your regular income taxes. Instead, to find out how much of your Social Security benefit is taxable, the Social Security Administration calculates it this way:

Provisional Income = Adjusted Gross Income + Nontaxable Interest + ½ of Social Security

See that piece about nontaxable interest? That generally means interest from government bonds and notes. It surprises many people that, although you may not pay taxes on those assets, their income will count against you when it comes to Social Security taxation.

Once you have figured out your provisional income (also called "combined income"), you can use the following chart to figure out your Social Security taxes.[33]

---

[32] Social Security Administration. "Social Security Benefit Amounts For The Surviving Spouse By Year Of Birth."
https://www.ssa.gov/planners/survivors/survivorchartred.html
[33] Social Security Administration. "Benefits Planner: Income Taxes and Your Social Security Benefits." https://www.ssa.gov/planners/taxes.html

Taxes on Social Security		
Provisional Income = Adjusted Gross Income + Nontaxable Interest + ½ of Social Security		
If you are ____ and your provisional income is____, then...		Uncle Sam will tax ___ of your Social Security
Single	Married, filing jointly	
Less than $25,000	Less than $32,000	0%
$25,000 to $34,000	$32,000 to $44,000	Up to 50%
More than $34,000	More than $44,000	Up to 85%

This is one more reason it may benefit you to work with financial and tax professionals: They can look at your entire financial picture to make your overall retirement plan as tax-efficient as possible—including your Social Security benefit.

One strategy may be to delay taking Social Security, thereby allowing it to grow. This might involve waiting until the age of seventy, when your Social Security maxes out, thus earning you a growth of 8 percent for every year past your FRA. However, when you choose to retire before seventy, an income gap is created from the foregone benefit. Money could be withdrawn from your IRAs to cover that gap, but that becomes a taxable event.

The good news is that those withdrawals reduce the sum and potentially mitigate what we call a "ticking tax time bomb" of Required Minimum Distributions from IRAs. We'll address RMDs in detail a bit later, but for now, consider the possibility that you might place yourself in a lower tax bracket when you finally do flip the switch on Social Security, thereby reducing the taxes you'll pay on RMDs.

Working and Social Security: The Earnings Test

If you haven't reached FRA, but you started your Social Security benefits and are still working, things get a little hairy.

Because you have started Social Security payments, the Social Security Administration will pay out your benefits (at that reduced rate, of course, because you haven't reached your FRA). Yet, because you are working, the organization must also withhold from your check to add to your benefits, which you are already collecting. See how this complicates matters?

To address the situation, the government has what is called the earnings test. For 2022, you can earn up to $19,560 without it affecting your Social Security check. But, for every $2 you earn past that amount, the Social Security Administration will withhold $1. The earnings test loosens in the year of your FRA; if you are reaching FRA in 2022, you can earn up to $51,960 before you run into the earnings test, and the government only withholds $1 for every $3 past that amount. The month you reach FRA, you are no longer subject to any earnings withholding. For instance, if you are still working and will turn sixty-six on December 28, 2022, you would only have to worry about the earnings test until December, and then you can ignore it entirely. Keep in mind, the money the government withholds from your Social Security benefits while you are working before FRA will be tacked back onto your benefits check after FRA.[34]

An important piece of a Retirement & Legacy Blueprint™ is to optimize Social Security timing. At Castle Wealth Group, we use sophisticated software to model various outcomes based on when our clients take Social Security. We are then able to assess the available options to help them determine what will work best for them.

---

34 Social Security Administration. "Exempt Amounts Under the Earnings Test." https://www.ssa.gov/oact/cola/rtea.html

Chapter 5: Social Security
KEY CONCEPTS

✓ Questions abound concerning the solvency of Social Security, but there has been no serious discussion about reneging on current obligations

✓ The Social Security Administration bases your monthly benefit on your earnings history and full retirement age (FRA).

✓ Social Security benefits are not necessarily tax-free.

Look Ahead. . .Chapter 6: 401(k)s & IRAs
Examining the rise of defined benefit plans (401(k)s, IRAs) and the decline of defined contribution plans (pensions).

401(k)s & IRAs

"Everyone's lost a lot of money on their 401(k) plans. I've heard some people calling them 201(k) plans. So it's even more important to get people to be saving more for retirement."
—*Richard Thaler*

Have you heard? Today's retirement is not your parents' retirement. You see, back in the day, it was pretty common to work for one company for the vast majority of your career and then retire with a gold watch and a pension.

The gold watch was a symbol of the quality time you had put in at that company, but the pension was more than a symbol. Instead, it was a guarantee—as solid as your employer—that they would repay your hard work with a certain amount of income in your old age. Did you see the caveat there? Your pension's guarantee was *as solid as your employer.* The problem was, what if your employer went under?

Companies that failed couldn't pay their retired employees' pensions, leading to financial challenges for many. Beginning in 1974 with Congress' passage of the Employee Retirement Income Security Act, federal legislation and regulations aimed at protecting retirees were everywhere. One piece of legislation included a relatively obscure section of the Internal Revenue Code, added in 1978. Section 401(k), to be specific.

IRC section 401, subsection k, created tax advantages for employer-sponsored financial products, even if the main contributor was the employee him or herself. Over the years, more employers took note, beginning an age of transition away from pensions and toward 401(k) plans. A 401(k) is a retirement account with certain tax benefits and restrictions on the investments or other financial products inside of it.

Essentially, 401(k)s and their individual retirement account (IRA) counterparts are "wrappers" that provide tax benefits around assets; typically, the assets that compose IRAs and 401(k)s are mutual funds, stock and bond mixes, and money market accounts. However, IRA and 401(k) contents are becoming more diverse these days, with some companies offering different kinds of annuity options within their plans.

Where pensions are defined-*benefit* plans, 401(k)s and IRAs are defined-*contribution* plans. The one-word change outlines the basic difference. Pensions spell out what you can expect to receive from the plan but not necessarily how much money it will take to fund those benefits. With 401(k)s, an employer sets a standard for how much they will contribute (if any), and you can be certain of what you are contributing. Still, there is no outline for what you can expect to receive in return for those contributions.

Modern employment looks very different. A 2018 survey by the Bureau of Labor Statistics determined U.S. workers stayed with their employers a median of about four years. Workers ages fifty-five to sixty-four had a little more staying power and were most likely to stay with their employer for about ten years.[35] Additionally, the outlook on the benefits front is different today, too. In 1979, 38 percent of workers had pensions. But 401(k)s are rising in number, with about 55 million American workers enrolled in a plan.[36]

A far cry from a pension and gold watch, wouldn't you say?

The old paradigm of retirement possibly resembles the working career of your grandparents or even your parents. That

[35] Bureau of Labor Statistics. September 20,2018. "Employee Tenure Summary." https://www.bls.gov/news.release/tenure.nr0.htm
[36] Investment Company Institute. December 31, 2018. "Frequently Asked Questions about 401(k) Plan Research." https://www.ici.org/policy/retirement/plan/401k/faqs_401k

norm found people working for one company their whole career before retiring. Pensions were far more prevalent than they are today, and when added to their Social Security and retirement savings, they provided an often sturdy "three-legged stool."

Now, however, with the evolution of the 401(k) and defined contribution plans, many employers have moved away from offering pensions, instead choosing to offer saving plans with company matching funds up to a certain percentage of an employee's contribution. The downside of employer-sponsored plans is that it places the onus on the retiree to manage these funds.

If there is anything to learn from this paradigm shift, it's that you must look out for yourself. Whether you have worked for a company for two years or twenty, you are still the one who has to look out for your own best interests. That holds doubly true when it comes to preparing for retirement. If you are one of the lucky ones who still has a pension, good for you. But for the rest of us, it is likely a 401(k)—or possibly one of its nonprofit- or government-sector counterparts, a 403(b) or 457 plan—is one of your biggest assets for retirement.

Some employers offer incentives to contribute to their company plans, like a company match. On that subject, I have one thing to say: *Do it!* Nothing in life is free, as they say, but a company match on your retirement funds is about as close to free money as it gets. If you can make the minimum to qualify for your company's match at all, go for it.

Now, it's likely, during our working years, we mostly "set and forget" our 401(k) funding. Because it is tax-advantaged, your employer is taking money from your paycheck—before taxes— and putting it into your plan for you. Maybe you got to pick a selection of investments, or maybe your company only offers one choice of investment in your 401(k). Either way, while you are gainfully employed, your most impactful decision may just be the decision to continue funding your plan in the first place. But, when you are ready to retire or move jobs, you have choices to make requiring a little more thought and care.

When you are ready to part ways with your job, you have a few options:

- Leave the money where it is
- Take the cash (and pay income taxes and perhaps a 10 percent additional federal tax if you are younger than age fifty-nine-and-one-half)
- Transfer the money to another employer plan (if the new plan allows)
- Roll the money over into a self-directed IRA

Now, these are just general options. You will have to decide, hopefully with the help of a financial professional, what's right for you. For instance, 401(k)s are typically pretty closely tied to the companies offering them, so when changing jobs, it may not always be possible to transfer a 401(k) to another 401(k). Leaving the money where it is may also be out of the question— some companies have direct cash payout or rollover policies once someone is no longer employed.

Also, remember what we said earlier about how we change jobs more often these days? That means you likely have a 401(k) with your current company, but you may also have a string of retirement accounts trailing you from other jobs.

In fact, I remember sitting down with a gentleman who had worked for seven employers throughout his lifetime and had six 401(k) plans in addition to the one with his current employer.

Portfolio rebalancing can be simplified when merging multiple 401(k) accounts. Simplification is also possible if accounts are consolidated once you reach the age of seventy-two and must begin taking required minimum distributions (RMDs).

However, don't correlate consolidation of 401(k) accounts as a measure that makes sense only for those who are nearing or in retirement. Stranded 401(k) funds can be an issue for younger workers, too, considering Americans over the age of twenty-five often move to a different job after about five years.[37]

One advantage to using the Retirement & Legacy Blueprint™ is the simplicity it provides in consolidating your accounts.

When it comes to your retirement income, it's important to be able to pull together *all* your assets, so you can examine what you have and where, and then decide what you will do with it.

Tax-Qualified, Tax-Preferred, Tax-Deferred … Still TAXED

Financial media often cite IRAs and 401(k)s for their tax benefits. After all, with traditional plans, you put your money in, pre-tax, and it hopefully grows for years, even decades, untaxed. That's why these accounts are called "tax-qualified" or "tax-deferred" assets. They aren't *tax-free!* Rarely does Uncle Sam allow business to continue without receiving his piece of the pie, and your retirement assets are no different. If you didn't pay taxes on the front end, you will pay taxes on the money you withdraw from these accounts in retirement. Don't get me wrong: This isn't an inherently good or bad thing; it's just the way it is. It's important to understand, though, for the sake of planning ahead.

In retirement, many people assume they will be in a lower tax bracket. Are you planning to pare down your lifestyle in retirement? Perhaps you are, and perhaps you will have substantially less income in retirement. But many of my clients tell me they want to live life more or less the same as they always have. The money they would previously have spent on business attire or gas for their commute they now want to spend on hobbies and grandchildren. That's all fine, and for many of

---

[37] Greg Iacurci. cnbc.com. December 31, 2019. "Why you should consolidate those 401(k)s and IRAs" https://www.cnbc.com/2019/12/31/why-you-should-consolidate-those-401ks-and-iras.html

them, it is doable, but does it put them in a lower tax bracket? Probably not.

Keep in mind, IRAs, 401(k)s, and their alternatives have a few limitations because of their special tax status. For one thing, the IRS sets limits on your contributions to these retirement accounts. If you are contributing to a 401(k) or an equivalent nonprofit or government plan, your annual contribution limit is $20,500 (as of 2022). If you are fifty or older, the IRS allows additional contributions, called "catch-up contributions," of up to $6,500 on top of the regular limit of $20,500. For an IRA, the limit is $7,000, with a catch-up limit of an additional $1,000. [38]

Because their tax advantages come from their intended use as retirement income, withdrawing funds from these accounts before you turn fifty-nine-and-one-half can carry stiff penalties. In addition to fees your investment management company might charge, you will have to pay income tax *and* a 10 percent federal tax penalty, with few exceptions.

The fifty-nine-and-one-half rule for retirement accounts is incredibly important to remember, especially when you're young. Younger workers are often tempted to cash out an IRA from a previous employer and then are surprised to find their checks missing 20 percent of the account value to income taxes, penalty taxes, and account fees.

Many millennials I see in my practice say, while they may be socking money away in their workplace retirement plan, it is often the *only* place they are saving. This could be problematic later because of the fifty-nine-and-one-half rule; what if you have an emergency? It is important to fund your retirement, but you need to have some liquid assets handy as emergency funds. This can help you avoid breaking into your retirement accounts and incurring taxes and penalties because of the fifty-nine-and-one-half rule.

---

[38] [38] Jackie Stewart. Kiplinger.com. Dec. 17, 2021. "401(k) Contribution Limits for 2022" https://www.kiplinger.com/retirement/retirement-plans/401ks/603949/401k-contribution-limits-for-2022

RMDs

Remember how we talked about the 401(k) or IRA being a "tax wrapper" for your funds? Well, eventually, Uncle Sam will want a bite of that candy bar. So, when you turn seventy-two, the government requires you withdraw a portion of your account, which the IRS calculates based on the size of your account and your estimated lifespan. This required minimum distribution, or RMD, is the government's insurance that it will collect some taxes, at some point, from your earnings. Because you didn't pay taxes on the front end, you will now pay income taxes on whatever you withdraw, including your RMDs. Also, let me just remind you not to play chicken with the U.S. government; if you don't take your RMDs starting at seventy-two, you will have to write a check to the IRS for *50 percent* of the amount of your missed RMDs. With the change in law from the SECURE Act of 2019, even after you begin RMDs, you can still also continue contributing to your 401(k) or IRAs if you are still employed, which can affect the whole discussion on RMDs and possible tax considerations.

If you don't need income from your retirement accounts, RMDs can seem like more of a tax burden than an income boon. While some people prefer to reinvest their RMDs, this comes with the possibility of additional taxation: You'll pay income taxes on your RMDs and then capital gains taxes on the growth of your investments. If you are legacy minded, there are other ways to use RMDs, many of which have tax benefits.

Permanent Life Insurance
One way to turn those pesky RMDs into a legacy is through permanent life insurance. Assuming you need the death benefit coverage and can qualify for it medically, if properly structured, these products can pass on a sizeable death benefit to your beneficiaries, tax-free, as part of your general legacy plan.

ILIT

Another way to use RMDs toward your legacy is to work with an estate planning attorney to create an irrevocable life insurance trust (ILIT). This is basically a permanent life insurance policy placed within a trust. Because the trust is irrevocable, you would relinquish control of it, but, unlike with just a permanent life insurance policy, your death benefit won't count toward your taxable estate.

Annuities

Because annuities can be tax-deferred, using all or a portion of your RMDs to fund an annuity contract can be one way to further delay taxation while guaranteeing your income payments (either to you or your loved ones) later. (Assuming you don't need the RMD income during your retirement.)

Qualified Charitable Distributions

If you are charity-minded, you may use your RMDs toward a charitable organization instead of using them for income. You must do this directly from your retirement account (you can't take the RMD check and *then* pay the charity) for your withdrawals to be qualified charitable distributions (QCDs), but this is one way of realizing some of the benefits of a charitable legacy during your own lifetime. You will not need to pay taxes on your QCDs, and they won't count toward your annual charitable tax deduction limit, plus you'll be able to see how the organization you are supporting uses your donations. You should consult a financial professional on how to correctly make a QCD, particularly since the SECURE Act of 2019 has implemented a few regulations on this point.[39]

When a person doesn't need the RMDs they are receiving as income, there are a variety of different planning strategies they

---

[39] Bob Carlson. Forbes. January 28, 2020. "More Questions And Answers About The SECURE Act."
https://www.forbes.com/sites/bobcarlson/2020/01/28/more-questions-and-answers-about-the-secure-act/#113d49564869

can use to meet their goals. A good place to start is to define their goals, develop a strategy, then pick the right tools, a process we manage at Castle Wealth Group to help tailor a plan that fits your needs.

For example, if a person with a $30,000 RMD has children and grandchildren they want to provide for, and the RMD is not needed as income, one option is to split the RMD so that it can be gifted. This can be done without incurring a tax, which the IRS imposes on gifts exceeding $15,000.[40] However, if we are optimizing a legacy, that RMD could be used to pay for a permanent life insurance policy (if you qualify medically and perhaps financially), thereby leaving the beneficiary a large lump sum of tax-free money. While the taxpayer who was imposed the RMD must still pay taxes, permanent life insurance will result in no tax consequence for a properly named beneficiary of an insurance policy.

Roth IRA

Since the Taxpayer Relief Act of 1997, there has been a different kind of retirement account, or "tax wrapper," available to the public: the Roth. Roth IRAs and Roth 401(k)s each differ from their traditional counterparts in one big way: You pay your taxes on the front end. This means, once your post-tax money is in the Roth account, as long as you follow the rules and limitations of that account, your distributions are truly tax-free. You won't pay income tax when you take withdrawals, so, in turn, you don't have to worry about RMDs. However, Roth accounts have the same limitations as traditional 401(k)s and IRAs when it comes to withdrawing money before age fifty-nine-and-one-half, with the added stipulation that the account

---

[40] Liz Smith. smartasset.com. November 5, 2020. "Gift Tax Limits: How Much Can You Gift?" https://smartasset.com/retirement/gift-tax-limits#:~:text=The%20IRS%20allows%20every%20taxpayer,lifetime%20exemption%20of%20%2411.58%20million

must have been open for at least five years in order for the accountholder to make withdrawals.

Every year, we engage our clients in a conversation regarding "Bracket Bumping," a term specific to managing Roth conversions. We look at what tax bracket clients are in and may recommend that they fill that bracket with Roth conversions or purchase an Indexed Universal Life Insurance (IUL) policy when it's appropriate for their situation. By doing so, we move money from the tax-deferred bucket to the tax-free bucket so that the client will have more tax-free income in retirement or be able to leave a tax-free inheritance.

Taking Charge

As mentioned earlier, the 401(k) and IRA have largely replaced pensions, but they aren't an equal trade.

Pensions are employer-funded; the money feeding into them is money that wouldn't ever show up on your pay stub. Because 401(k)s are self-funded, you must actively and consciously save. This distinction has made a difference when it comes to funding retirement. According to one NerdWallet article, the average 401(k) balance for a person age sixty to sixty-nine is $198,600, but the median likely tells the full story. The median 401(k) balance for a person age sixty to sixty-nine is $63,000. The article also cites the general suggestion to aim, by age thirty, to have saved up an amount equal to 50 percent to 100 percent of your annual salary.[41] For some thirty-year-olds, saving half an annual salary by age thirty is more than some sixty-to-sixty-nine-year-olds have saved for their entire lives

There can be many reasons why people underfund their retirement plans, like being overwhelmed by the investment choices or taking withdrawals from IRAs when they leave an

---

[41] Arielle O'Shea. Nerd Wallet. January 24, 2019. "The Average 401(k) Balance by Age." https://www.nerdwallet.com/article/investing/the-average-401k-balance-by-age

employer, but the reason at the top of the list is this: People simply aren't participating to begin with.

So, whether you use a 401(k) with an employer or an IRA alternative with a private company, separate from your workplace, the most important retirement savings decision you can make is to sock away your money somewhere in the first place.

Chapter 6: 401(k)s & IRAs
KEY CONCEPTS

✓   Contributing enough to qualify for a full company match on the retirement plan it offers closely equates to free money

✓   Withdrawing funds from IRAs and 401(k)s before turning fifty-nine-and-one-half can result in stiff penalties

✓   The IRS collects taxes on your 401(k) or IRA account when you turn seventy-two by collecting mandatory withdrawals called required minimum distributions (RMDs)

Look Ahead. . .Chapter 7: Annuities
Annuities sometimes seem to be shrouded in mystery and deserve closer inspection.

CHAPTER 7
Annuities

"An Annuity is very serious business"
—Jane Austen

In my practice, I offer my clients a variety of products—from securities to insurance—all designed to help them reach their financial goals. You may be wondering: Why single out a single product in this book?

Well, while most of my clients have a pretty good understanding of business and finance, I sometimes find those who have the impression there must be magic involved. Some people assume there is a magic finance wand we can wave to change years' worth of savings into a strategy for retirement income. But it's not as easy as a goose laying golden eggs or the Fairy Godmother turning a pumpkin into a coach!

Finances aren't magic; it takes lots of hard work and, typically, several financial products and strategies to pull together a complete retirement plan. Of all the financial products I work with, it seems people find none more mysterious than annuities. And, if I may say, even some of those who recognize the word "annuity" have a limited understanding of the product. So, in the interest of demystifying annuities, let me tell you a little about what an annuity is.

In general, insurance is a financial hedge against risk. Car owners buy auto insurance to protect their finances in case they injure someone, or someone injures them. Homeowners have house insurance to protect their finances in case of a fire, flood, or another disaster. People have life insurance to protect their finances in case of untimely death. Almost juxtaposed to life insurance, people have annuities in case of a long life; annuities can give you financial protection by providing consistent and reliable income payments.

The basic premise of an annuity is you, the annuitant, pay an insurance company some amount in exchange for their contractual guarantee they will pay you income for a certain time period. How that company pays you, for how long, and how much they offer are all determined by the annuity contract you enter into with the insurance company.

How You Get Paid

There are two ways for an annuity contract to provide income: The first is through what is called annuitization, and the second is through the use of income riders. We'll get into income riders in a bit, but let's first address annuitization. That nice, long word is, in my opinion, one reason annuities have a reputation for mystery and misinformation.

Annuitization

When someone "annuitizes" a contract, it is the point where he or she turns on the income stream. Once a contract has been annuitized, there is no going back. With annuities, if the policyholder lives longer than the insurance company planned, the insurance company is still obligated to pay him or her, even if the payments end up being way more than the contract's actual value. If, however, the policyholder dies an untimely death, depending on the contract type, the insurance company may keep anything left of the money that funded the annuity—nothing would be paid out to the contract holder's survivors. You see where that could make some people balk? Now, modern annuities rarely rely on annuitization for the income portion of the contract, and instead have so many bells and whistles that the old concept of annuitization seems outdated, but because this is still an option, it's important to at least understand the basic concept.

Riders

Speaking of bells and whistles, let's talk about riders. Modern annuities have a lot of different options these days, many in the form of riders you can add to your contract for a fee—usually about 1 percent of the contract value per year. Each rider has its particulars, and the types of riders available will vary by the type of annuity contract purchased, but I'll just briefly outline some of these little extras:

- Lifetime income rider: Contract guarantees you an enhanced income for life
- Death benefit rider: Contract pays an enhanced death benefit to your beneficiaries even if you have annuitized
- Return of premium rider: Guarantees you (or your beneficiaries) will at least receive back the premium value of the annuity
- Long-term care rider: Provides a certain amount, sometimes as much as twice the principal value of the contract, to help pay for long-term care if the contract holder is moved to a nursing home or assisted living situation

This isn't an extensive look, and usually the riders have fancier names based on the issuing company, like "Lorem Ipsum Insurance Company Income Preferred Bonus Fixed Index Annuity rider," but I just wanted to show you what some of the general options are in layperson's terms.

Types of Annuities

Annuities break down into four basic types: immediate, variable, fixed, and fixed index.

Immediate

Immediate annuities primarily rely on annuitization to provide income—you give the insurance company a lump sum up front, and your payments begin immediately. Once you begin receiving income payments, the transaction is irreversible, and you no longer have access to your money in a lump sum. When you die, any remaining contract value is typically forfeited to the insurance company.

All other annuity contract types are "deferred" contracts, meaning you fund your policy as a lump sum or over a period of years and you give it the opportunity to grow over time—sometimes years, sometimes decades.

Variable

A variable annuity is an insurance contract as well as an investment. It's sold by insurance companies, but only through someone who is registered to sell investment products. With a variable annuity contract, the insurance company invests your premiums in subaccounts that are tied to the stock market. This makes it a bit different from the other annuity contract types because it is the only contract where your money is subject to losses because of market declines. Your contract value has a greater opportunity to grow, but it also stands to lose. Additionally, your contract's value will be subject to the underlying investment's fees and limitations—including capital gains taxes, management fees, etc. Once it is time for you to receive income from the contract, the insurance company will pay you a certain income, locked in at whatever your contract's value was.

Variable annuities seem to garner a lot of bad press and often leave people with a bad impression until they gain a better understanding of their uses and benefits in certain situations. For instance, variable annuities typically have higher fees than other types—strike one. Variable annuities can lose their cash value—strike two. Variable annuities often have high commission structures—that's strike three. But to their credit, they also have the potential for higher returns than any other type of annuity. In addition, you can purchase optional riders for added protection. In general, variable annuities tend to be more appropriate for younger investors who have the time and risk appetite to sustain potential losses in exchange for the opportunity for higher returns.

But it's important to understand not all annuities are alike. The negative feelings people have often stem from seeing variable types and fixed index types as one in the same.

Fixed

A traditional fixed annuity is pretty straightforward. You purchase a contract with a guaranteed interest rate and, when you are ready, the insurance company will make regular income payments to you at whatever payout rate your contract guarantees. Those payments will continue for the rest of your life and, if you choose, for the remainder of your spouse's life.

Fixed annuities don't have much in the way of upside potential, but many people like them for their guarantees (after all, if your Aunt May lives to be ninety-five, knowing she has a paycheck later in life can be her mental and financial safety net), as well as for their predictability. Unlike variable annuities, which are subject to market risk and might be up one year and down the next, you can easily calculate the value of your fixed annuity over your lifetime.

Fixed Index

To recap, variable annuities take on more risk to offer more possibilities to grow. Fixed annuities have less potential growth, but they protect your principal. In the last couple of decades, many insurance companies have retooled their product line to offer fixed index annuities, which are sort of midway between variable and fixed annuities on that risk/reward spectrum. Fixed index annuities offer greater growth potential than traditional fixed annuities but less than variable annuities. Like traditional fixed annuities, however, fixed index annuities are protected from downside market losses.

Fixed index annuities earn interest that is tied to the market, meaning that, instead of your contract value growing at a set interest rate like a traditional fixed annuity, it has the potential to grow within a range. Your contract's value is credited interest based on the performance of an external market index like the S&P 500. However, it is never invested in the market itself. You can't invest in the S&P 500 directly, but each year, your annuity has the potential to earn interest based on the chosen index's performance. This it is subjected to limits set by the company such as caps, spreads and participation rates. For instance, if your contract caps your interest at 5 percent, then in a year that the S&P 500 gains 3 percent, your annuity value increases 3 percent. If the S&P 500 gains 35 percent, your annuity value gets a 5 percent interest bump. But since your money isn't actually invested in the market with a fixed index annuity, if the market nosedives (such as happened during 2000, 2008 and 2020, anyone?) you won't see any increase in your contract value. Conversely, there will also be no decrease in your contract value—no matter how badly the market performed, as long as you follow the terms of the contract, you won't lose any of the interest you were credited in previous years.

So, what if the S&P 500 shows a market loss of 30 percent? Your contract value isn't going anywhere (unless you purchased an optional rider—this charge will still come out of your annuity value each year). For those who are more interested in protection than growth potential, fixed index annuities can be an attractive option because, when the stock market has a long period of positive performance, a fixed index annuity can enjoy conservative growth. And, during stretches where the stock market is erratic and stock values across the board take significant losses? Fixed index annuities won't lose anything due to the stock market volatility.

There are some retirement planning strategies, depending on your goals, where a fixed index annuity may be the right tool to use.

First, fixed index annuities can be a good tool for accumulation and growth, where your principal is protected against the downside, but can still collect a portion of the upside through interest credits.

They can also work well for many because they create an income flow in the future. There are two main ways this can happen. The simplest way is a "drawdown" strategy. Let's say, someone retired at sixty-two and wants to delay taking Social Security so that they allow it to grow. How will their income gap be covered? If they draw down their assets in the market, they may be subject to Sequence of Return Risk, potentially causing their market assets to drop. There is often not enough time to make up losses based on a person's earning potential and ability to contribute to a market-driven retirement account. But, by drawing from a vehicle with principal protection, they shielded themselves from Sequence of Return Risk and created a steady stream of predictable income, ideally until their Social Security is turned on.

A second way to use fixed index annuities for income would be to 'annuitize" the annuity at a future time. Based on the amount saved and the pay-out factor, you can guarantee a lifetime income for you or you and a spouse.

A third benefit of fixed index annuities, in addition to growth and income, is a long-term care hedge. There are certain annuities that offer long-term care benefits if assistance is needed with daily living activities and typically there is no underwriting. If you have a loved one diagnosed with Alzheimer's and care will be needed in the future, a FIA with a long-term care rider could be purchased to leverage funds to pay for it. One caveat is that with some FIAs, as part of the annuity contract, you must go two years without triggering the long-term care payout. So, consider an FIA as a long-term care insurance strategy if you cannot qualify for long-term care insurance.

The fourth strategy to consider with an FIA is to use it as a legacy enhancer. Let's say you are not planning on using the money in your lifetime and want to leave more to the next generation and, because of age or health, permanent life insurance is not an option. Instead, a legacy FIA, which could provide a percentage of the annuity's value to beneficiaries upon death, may be an option.

Other Things to Know About Annuities

We just talked about the four kinds of annuity contracts available, but all of them have some commonalities as annuities.

For all annuities, the contractual guarantees are only as strong as the insurance company that sells the product, which makes it important to thoroughly check the credit ratings of any company whose products you are considering.

Annuities are tax-deferred, meaning you don't have to pay taxes on interest earnings each year as the contract value grows. Instead, you will pay ordinary income taxes on your withdrawals. These are meant to be long-term products, so, like other tax-deferred or tax-advantaged products, if you begin taking withdrawals from your contract before age fifty-nine-and-one-half, you may also have to pay a 10 percent federal tax penalty. Also, while annuities are generally considered illiquid, most contracts allow you to withdraw up to 10 percent of your contract value every year. Withdraw any more, however, and you could incur additional surrender penalties.

Keep in mind, your withdrawals will deplete the accumulated cash value, death benefit, and, possibly, the rider values of your contract.

Annuities aren't for everyone, but it's important to understand them before saying "yea" or "nay" on whether they fit into your plan; otherwise, you're not operating with complete information, wouldn't you agree? Regardless, you should talk to a financial professional who can help you understand annuities, help you dissect your particular financial needs, and help show you whether an annuity is appropriate for your retirement income plan.

Chapter 7: Annuities
KEY CONCEPTS

✓ Annuities can provide financial protection by offering consistent and reliable income payments

✓ Contractual guarantees are only as strong as the insurance company that sells the product

✓ Four basic types of annuities—immediate, variable, fixed, and fixed index—contain different components and attributes

Look Ahead. . .Chapter 8: Estate & Legacy
Choosing the right tools and aligning them with your estate and legacy goals can reduce burdens faced by grieving loved ones.

CHAPTER 8

Estate & Legacy

"He that hath a Trade, hath an Estate."
—Benjamin Franklin

In my practice, I devote a significant portion of my time to matters of estates. That includes drawing up wills or trusts, putting together powers of attorney, or other legal documents. After all, I'm a Certified Elder Law Attorney®. Estate and legacy planning isn't just about using wills and trusts—there's more to it. Those are just tools. What's more important is choosing the right tools and aligning them with your estate and legacy goals.

I've included this chapter because I have seen so many people do estate planning incorrectly. Clients, or clients' families, have come in after experiencing a death in the family and have found themselves in the middle of probate, high taxes, or a discovery of something unforeseen (often long-term care) draining the estate.

I have also seen people do estate planning right: clients or families who visit my office to talk about legacies and how to make them last and adult children who have room to grieve without an added burden of unintended costs, without stress from a family ruptured because of inadequate planning.

I'll share some of these stories here. However, I'm not going to give you specific advice, since everyone's situation is unique.

95

I only want to give you some things to think about and to underscore the importance of planning ahead.

As a Certified Elder Law Attorney (CELA®), I focus on more than what happens if you pass away; that's estate planning. I became a CELA® because I found early in my practice, people were not passing away. Rather, they were continuing to age and face all the issues that go along with aging. I focus on what happens if you continue living. I focus on helping make sure your money lasts as long as you do.

When we talk about estate planning, legacy, and elder care, there are certain legal tools that are typically used to make up an estate plan. Those tools are:

- Trust (either a living trust or a Castle Trust™)
- Last Will and Testament
- Financial Power of Attorney
- Medical Power of Attorney
- Personal Care Plan
- Final Expense Tool

I'll go over these documents in more detail.

By working with an estate planner or attorney, or in my case, a Certified Elder Law Attorney®, you can find out how these tools can be used to strategically help you meet your estate and legacy planning goals.

You Can't Take It With You

When it comes to legacy and estate planning, the most important thing is to DO IT. I have heard my clients, as well as some celebrities, say they aren't interested in what happens to their assets when they die because they will be dead. Snoop Dogg is someone who comes to mind for mentioning this. That's certainly one way to look at it. But I think that's a very selfish way to go about things—we all have people and causes we care about, and those who care about us. Even if the people we love don't *need* what we leave behind, they can still be fined or legally tied up in the probate process or burial costs if we don't plan for those. And that's not even considering what happens if you become incapacitated at some point while you are still alive. Having a plan in place can greatly reduce the stress of those responsibilities on your loved ones; it's just a loving thing to do.

Documents

There are a few documents that lay the groundwork of legacy planning. You've probably heard of all or most of them, but I'd like to review what they are and how people commonly use them. These are all things you should talk about with an estate planning attorney to establish your legacy.

Powers of Attorney

A power of attorney, or POA, is a document giving someone the authority to act on your behalf and in your best interests. These come in handy in situations where you cannot be present (think a vacation where you get stuck in Canada) or, for durable powers of attorney, even when you are incapacitated (think in a coma or coping with dementia).

It is important to have powers of attorney in place and to appoint someone you trust to act on your behalf in these matters. Have you ever heard of someone who was incapacitated after a car accident, whether from head trauma or being in a coma for weeks—sometimes months? Do you think their bills stopped coming due during that time? I like my phone company and my bank, but neither one is about to put a moratorium on sending me bills, particularly not for an extended or interminable period. A power of attorney would have the authority to pay your mortgage or cancel your cable while you are unable.

You can have multiple POAs
and require them to act jointly.

What this looks like: Do you think two heads are better than one? One man, Chris, significantly relied on his two sons' opinions for both his business and personal matters. He appointed both sons as joint POA, requiring both their signoffs for his medical and financial matters.

You can have multiple POAs
who can act independently.

What this looks like: Irene had three children with whom she routinely stayed. They lived in different areas of the country, which she thought was an advantage; one month she might be hiking out West, the next she could enjoy the newest off-Broadway production, and the next she could soak up some Southern sun. She named her three children as independently authorized POAs, so, if something happened, no matter where she was, the child closest could step in to act on her behalf.

You can have POAs who have
different responsibilities.

What this looks like: Although Luke's friend Claire, a nurse, was his go-to and POA for health-related issues, financial matters usually made her nervous, so he appointed his good neighbor, Matt, as his POA in all of his financial and legal matters.

In addition to POAs, it may be helpful to have an advanced medical directive. This is a document where you have pre-decided what choices you would make about different health scenarios. An advanced medical directive can help ease the burden for your medical POA and loved ones, particularly when it comes to end-of-life care.

The two most common POAs I work with are financial and medical POAs. Both appoint a designated person (not necessarily the same person) to make decisions either about your financial or medical matters, should you become incapable. A medical POA includes end-of-life decisions.

A disability document is a third POA that gives instructions to the financial power and medical power about a person's personal care plan. Whereas the medical power of attorney addresses end-of-life decision-making, the disability document addresses long-term care decisions.

We will sit down with you and spend the time to review these options to determine the best that fits your individual needs.

Wills

Perhaps the most basic document of legacy planning, a will is a legal document wherein you outline your wishes for your estate. When it comes to your estate after your death, having a will is the foundation of your legacy. Without one, your loved ones are left behind, guessing what you would have wanted, and the court will likely split your assets according to the state's defaults. Maybe that's exactly what you wanted, as far as anyone knows, right? Because even if you told your nephew he could have your car he's been driving, if it's not in writing, it still might go to the brother, sister, son, or daughter to whom you aren't speaking.

However, it may not be enough just to have a will. Even with a will, your assets will be subject to probate. Probate is what we call the state's process for determining a will's validity. A judge will go through your will to question if it conflicts with state law, if it is the most up-to-date document, if you were mentally competent at the time it was in order, etc. For some, this is a quick, easily-resolved process. For others, particularly if someone steps forward to contest the will, it may take years to settle, all the while subjecting the assets to court costs and attorney's fees.

One other undesirable piece of the probate process is that it is a public process. That means anyone can go to the courthouse, ask for copies of the case, and discover your assets. They can also see who is slated to receive what and who is disputing.

I once sat down with the son of a doctor to discuss his father's estate plan, which had no trust, but only a will. His father, who had recently passed away, had a successful practice, with everything going to his wife and then to his son.

Because wills only serve as instructions to a probate court, the doctor's practice had to be sorted out legally. The wife had to pay $50,000 in probate fees to transfer ownership of the practice to another doctor.

All of that could have easily been avoided had the doctor funded his practice into a trust rather than just using a will. Remember, choosing the right tools for your estate is only decided after determining your goals.

It's also important to remember beneficiary lines trump wills. So, that large life insurance policy? What if, when you bought it fifteen years ago, you wrote your ex-husband's name on the beneficiary line? Even if you stipulate otherwise in your will, the company that holds your policy will pay out to your ex-spouse. Or, how about the thousands of dollars in your IRA you dedicated to the children thirty years ago, but one of your children was killed in a car accident, leaving his wife and two toddlers behind? That IRA is going to transfer to your remaining children, with nothing for your daughter-in-law and grandchildren.

That may paint a grim portrait, but I can't underscore enough the importance of working with a skilled estate planning attorney to keep your will and beneficiary lines up to date as your life changes, for the sake of your loved ones.

When I was twelve years old, my uncle passed away. He had worked on an assembly line at the Ford Motor Company, where he sustained a serious back injury, causing him to go on disability. Unfortunately, he became addicted to painkillers and died from an overdose, leaving three adult sons as his heirs. He had prepared a simple will indicating that everything should be split equally between them.

He didn't have much when he died, basically just a $10,000 life insurance policy that listed the youngest son as the sole beneficiary.

Where do you think the proceeds of the life insurance policy went? To the youngest son per the beneficiary designation, or to the three sons equally? Sadly, it became a huge fight that almost turned violent and thirty years later, they still don't talk to each other.

The $10,000 ultimately went to the youngest child because the will only controlled what was in probate. Since there was a beneficiary, the life insurance never made it to probate and therefore went to the youngest child.

Having his family break up over a $10,000 life insurance policy is definitely not what my uncle wanted. This unfortunate situation prompted me to help other families avoid such events. I joined the legal profession to help other families avoid the disruption potentially caused by lack of proper planning. With the combination of unique legal instruments, like Castle Trusts™, financial/income planning, and tax planning, we help families protect and preserve their legacies.

Legacy is not just about leaving a boatload of money to the next generation; it's about how you will be remembered. The tools we use help protect that legacy.

Trusts

Another piece of legacy planning to consider is the trust.

A trust is set up through an attorney and allows a third party, or trustee, to hold your assets and determine how they will pass to your beneficiaries. Many people are skeptical of trusts because they assume trusts are only appropriate for the fabulously wealthy.

However, a simple trust may only cost $3,000 to $5,500 in attorney's fees and can avoid both the expense and publicity of probate, provide a more immediate transfer of wealth, avoid some taxes, and provide you greater control over your legacy.[42]

---

[42] Regan Rondinelli-Haberek. LegalZoom. "What is the Average Cost to Prepare a Living Trust?" https://info.legalzoom.com/average-cost-prepare-living-trust-26932.html

There are also more complicated trusts, such as Legacy Trusts, Castle Trusts™, Irrevocable Trusts, and Estate Tax Planning Trusts.

For instance, if you want to set aside some funds for a grandchild's college education, you can make it a requirement he or she enrolls in classes before your trust will dispense any funds. Like a will, beneficiary lines will override your trust conditions, so you must still keep insurance policies and other assets up to date.

Like any financial or legal consideration, there are many options these days beyond the simple "yes or no" question of whether to have a trust. For one thing, you will need to consider if you want your trust to be revocable (you can change the terms while you are alive) or a Castle Trust™ (which avoids probate, protects the beneficiaries, and most importantly protects you). A brief note here about trusts: revocable living trusts avoid probate and can control the distribution upon death; however, they offer you zero asset protection. This is why many people look to Castle Trusts™ as a tool that can be used to avoid probate, protect their beneficiaries, and most importantly, protect against the high cost of long-term care by starting the five-year lookback period for Medicaid.

Another thing to remember when it comes to trusts, in general, is, even if you have set up a trust, you must remember to fund it. In my fifteen-plus years of work, I've had numerous clients come to me, assuming they have protected their assets with a trust. When we talk about taxes and other pieces of their legacy, it turns out they never retitled any assets or changed any paperwork on the assets they wanted in the trust. So, please remember, a trust is just a bunch of fancy legal papers if you haven't followed through on retitling your assets. At Castle Wealth Group, we work with our clients to help them get all of their assets funded correctly.

Taxes

Although charitable contributions, trusts, and other tax-efficient strategies can reduce your tax bill, it's unlikely your estate will be passed on entirely tax-free. Yet, when it comes to building a legacy that can last for generations, taxes can be one of the heaviest drains on the impact of your hard work.

For 2017, the federal estate exemption was $5.49 million per individual and $10.98 million for a married couple, with estates facing up to a 40 percent tax rate after that. In 2021, those limits increased to $11.7 million for individuals and $23.4 million for married couples, with the 40 percent top level gift and estate tax remaining the same. Currently, the new estate limits are set to increase with inflation until January 1, 2026, when they will "sunset" back to the inflation-adjusted 2017 limits.[43] And that's not taking into account the various state regulations and taxes regarding estate and inheritance transfers.

Another tax concern "frequent flyer": retirement accounts.

Your IRA or 401(k) can be a source of tax issues when you pass away. For one thing, taking funds from a sizeable account can trigger a large tax bill. However, if you leave the assets in the account, there are still required minimum distributions (RMDs), which will take effect even after you die. If you pass the account to your spouse, he or she can keep taking your RMDs as is, or your spouse can retitle the account in his or her name and receive RMDs based on his or her life expectancy. Remember, if you don't take your RMDs, the IRS will take up to 50 percent of whatever your required distribution was, plus you will still have to pay income taxes whenever you withdraw that money. Thanks to rules enacted in 2020, anyone who inherits your IRA, with few exceptions (your spouse, a

---

[43] Laura Sanders, Richard Rubin. The Wall Street Journal. April 8, 2021. "Estate and Gift Taxes 2020-2021: Here's What You Need to Know" https://www.wsj.com/articles/estate-and-gift-taxes-2020-2021-heres-what-you-need-to-know-11617908256

beneficiary less than ten years younger, or a disabled adult child, to name a few), will need to empty the account within ten years of your death.[44]

Also—and this is a pretty big also—check with an attorney if you are considering putting your IRA or 401(k) in a trust. An improperly titled beneficiary form for the IRA could mean the difference of thousands of dollars in taxes. As a financial professional, estate planning attorney and Certified Elder Law attorney, I can diligently check your decisions to help strategically structure your legacy planning.

Legacy planning is all about discovering your goals, developing strategies to help achieve those goals, and picking the right tools. Sometimes people come into our office and say they want a will-based estate plan, or a trust-based estate plan, or a Castle Trust™. We typically tell them to slow down a bit so we can first figure out what they are trying to accomplish. Whether to use a trust is not so much about net worth or assets (though these can play a role), but more about creating a plan that achieves success regardless of the circumstances.

For example, if you are looking to protect your children from high probate fees but you are not concerned about long-term care costs or lawsuits, then a revocable trust with legacy provisions for the children may make sense.

On the other hand, if you're concerned about long-term care costs, then you may be more interested in a Castle Trust™ that can help protect against nursing home costs by starting the five-year Medicaid lookback clock.

Either way, it starts with identifying your estate and legacy planning goals. A successful plan does not break up a family, such as the legacy left by my uncle.

---

[44] Julia Kagan. Investopedia. October 11, 2020. "Stretch IRA" https://www.investopedia.com/terms/s/stretch-ira.asp

Chapter 8: Estate & Legacy
KEY CONCEPTS

✓ An essential step related to estate planning is to do it. Reduce stress caused by responsibilities for your loved ones

✓ Taxes can be one of the biggest drains on the hard work you put in to build a legacy

✓ Many look to Castle Trusts™ as a tool to avoid probate, protect their beneficiaries, and most importantly, protect against the high cost of long-term care by starting the five-year lookback period for Medicaid

Look Ahead. . .Chapter 9: Indexed Universal Life Insurance
Understand the components of a life insurance product that could fortify your financial arsenal but is not suitable for everyone.

Indexed Universal Life Insurance

"To carry adequate life insurance is a moral obligation incumbent upon the great majority of citizens."
—*Franklin D. Roosevelt.*

My clients are not typically gamblers. A day at the casino is more likely to give them nightmares than it is to make them eager with dollar signs in their eyes. Many would rather work with at least some guarantees than with primarily stocks and risk-based products, so, of course, that often means turning more toward life insurance, and often to a product called indexed universal life insurance, also commonly referred to as fixed indexed universal life insurance. If you've never heard of that before, I'm not surprised. This life insurance product isn't suitable for everyone, but I want to take a second to talk about it because, for the right person, it can be a significant product in their financial arsenal.

Insurance: The Basics

If you haven't been casting around in the life insurance pond much, then let's take a second to cover the basics. During our working lives, it's likely we have some kind of basic term life policy, either privately or through our employers. Term life insurance means an individual is protected for a certain period of time—usually ten to thirty years. It typically correlates to a certain amount of wages (if it's an employer's plan) or a coverage amount chosen by the individual (if it's a person's private insurance). At its most basic, term insurance provides funds for our loved ones and can be used for a number of purposes, including covering funeral expenses or something of that nature. Oftentimes, people will take out more than this—for instance, families with a stay-at-home parent sometimes purchase policies based on the working parent's life to cover years of income, plus the mortgage, etc. Your premium for a term life policy will be based on things like your coverage limit, your age, your health, and the term of the policy. The older you are, the more likely it is you have health events or other issues that could make it more difficult to obtain term life insurance and the more expensive it is. Some consumers may see this as a disadvantage of term life insurance because they pay into a policy for twenty years, and then it reaches its "endowment"— the end of the contract term—and there are no additional benefits.

Permanent Insurance

Aside from the basic term life policies many wage-earners hold, insurance companies also have permanent policies, also sometimes referred to as "cash value insurance." With a permanent insurance contract, your policy will typically remain in force as long as you continue to keep it funded (there is an exception for whole life policies, which we'll get to later). A permanent insurance contract has two pieces: the death benefit and cash value accumulation. Both are spelled out in your contract. As these products gained recognition, people began to realize the products had significant advantages when it came to taxes. I don't really want to get too technical, but it is really the technical details that make these policies valuable to their owners. That bit about tax advantages makes permanent life insurance policies attractive to consumers because, not only do they receive an income-tax-free death benefit for their beneficiaries, they may also be able to borrow against their policy, income-tax-free, if they end up needing the money.

For example, let's say Emma purchases a life insurance policy when she's thirty. She hates the idea of not having anything to show for her premiums over ten to twenty years, so she decides to use a permanent policy. Then, when she's close to fifty, her brother finds himself in dire straits. Emma wants to help, and she's been a diligent saver. The catch is most of her money is in products like her 401(k) or an annuity. These may be fabulous products suitable for her needs, but her circumstance has just changed, and she's looking for ways to help her sibling without incurring significant tax penalties. But wait . . . she has that permanent life insurance policy! She can borrow any accumulated cash value against her policy, free of income taxes. So, let's say she borrows a few thousand dollars from her policy. She doesn't have to pay taxes on any of it. She can pay it back into her policy at any time. Then, let's say Emma dies before she "settles up" her policy (or pays back that loan). As long as she continued paying premium payments or otherwise kept her policy adequately funded until she died, then her beneficiaries will still receive a death benefit, minus the policy loan.

Are you with me so far? Here are the central themes on properly structured permanent life insurance policies: tax-free death benefit and income-tax-free withdrawals through policy loans are available as long as the premiums continue to be paid, and a minimum rate of cash value accumulation is guaranteed by the strength of the insurer.

Now, let's dive a little deeper into the two basic categories of permanent insurance on the market: whole life policies and universal life policies.

Whole Life Insurance

With whole life, an actuary in a back office has calculated what a person your age with your intended death benefit coverage, your health history, your potential lifespan—and other minutia—should pay for a premium rate. Depending on how the insurer's rate tables are calculated, your whole life policy will "endow" at a certain age—ninety, one hundred, one hundred twenty, etc.—so there is the risk you could outlive the policy, and the death benefit would pay out to you instead of your beneficiaries, which may create unplanned tax consequences. Nonetheless, to qualify for your whole life policy, you will complete a medical questionnaire and possibly a paramedical exam, and then, based on that information, an underwriter will place you in one of these actuarial categories to determine your premium rate. One benefit of whole life insurance is the insurance company will credit a certain amount back into the policy's cash value based on your contract's guaranteed rate. Some insurance companies may also pay a dividend back to policyholders at the company's discretion.

Take Emma from the preceding example, and let's consider the scenario if her permanent insurance policy was a whole life policy. When she first purchased the contract, the insurance agent would have been able to tell her what her locked-in premium rate would be. She would pay the same amount, year after year, to keep her contract in force. And she could also calculate her policy's minimum cash value to the penny.

Universal Life Insurance

If whole life is the basic permanent life insurance policy, universal is the souped-up model. It has eight speeds, comes in many different colors, and has more options, which also means it might take some extra time and research to be thoroughly understood. But this means, if it's right for you, it can be even more customizable and fine-tuned to your specific needs.

The major differences:
- Flexible premium
- Increasing policy costs

Let's start with those increasing policy costs. Basically, the internal cost to the insurance company of maintaining your policy will increase over time, like a term insurance policy. Remember how whole life policies have those actuaries at the insurer's office calculating all of that and then determining a set rate for you to pay to cover it all? Well, with universal life, that's part of the flexible premium part. You can decide to pay a premium that will cover your future policy expenses, or you can decide to pay a premium that barely covers your current policy expenses, depending on your circumstances.

That is where these policies have gotten a bad rap in the past. If you purchase a policy and only ever pay the minimum premium required, your policy could end up losing value to the point your premium no longer covers your policy's expenses, and then the policy would lapse. That's also why it's incredibly important to work with a financial professional you trust, who can shoot straight about whether this kind of product would be appropriate for you and who makes sure you fully understand all the details.

To return to our example of Emma, though, here's how a well-set-up universal life insurance policy could work: Emma, ever the diligent saver, would have paid well over the minimum premium every month. Every time she got a raise or payroll increase, she increased the amount of premium she paid into her policy. With the policy's contractual rate of interest, she had a substantial amount of cash value accumulated in the policy. That way, when she decided to borrow money against the policy to help her brother, she could even afford to decrease her monthly payments for a time, until she was back in a better financial position.

Indexing

Now to the main event: *indexed* universal life insurance, or IUL. Like any permanent insurance, an IUL policy will remain in force as long as you continue to pay sufficient premiums, and you can borrow against your policy's cash value, income-tax-free. And, IUL policies are, at their core, universal life policies with that flexible premium. So, how are they different?

If you skim back through some of the other policy details, I covered the ability to withdraw the cash value of your policy without paying income taxes, even on the accumulation. Because of the index part of IULs, that accumulating cash value has the potential to accumulate more. An index is a tool that measures the movement of the market, like the S&P 500, or the Dow Jones Industrial Average. You can't invest directly in an index, it's just a sort of ruler. With an IUL policy, your cash accumulation interest credits are based on an index, with what is called a "floor" and a "cap" or other limits such as a spread or participation rate.

That means, if the market does well, each year your policy has the opportunity to be credited interest on the cash accumulation based on whatever your policy's index is, subject to the cap, spread or participation rate. If the market has a bad year and the index shows negative gains, your account still gets credited whatever your contract floor is. So, for example, let's say your contract cap is 12.5 percent and the floor is 0 percent. If the market returns 20 percent, your contract value gets a 12.5 percent interest credit. The next year, the S&P 500 returns a negative 26 percent. The insurance company won't credit your policy anything, but you also won't see your policy value slip because of that negative performance (although policy charges and expenses will still be deducted from your policy).

So, your policy won't lose value because of poor market conditions, but you can still stand to realize interest credits due to changes in an index. The following chart illustrates how an IUL works using the S&P 500. As you can see, because of the cap, the IUL doesn't have the sharp upticks of the index, but it also never goes down due to market losses. The potential cash accumulation is a real draw here for people who want protection from market losses, potential interest growth, and a death benefit for their beneficiaries. Some people also prefer to overfund their policies and borrow against their cash values to help provide supplemental retirement income. Keep in mind, policy loans will reduce available cash values and death benefits and may cause the policy to lapse, potentially requiring additional premium payments to keep the policy in force.

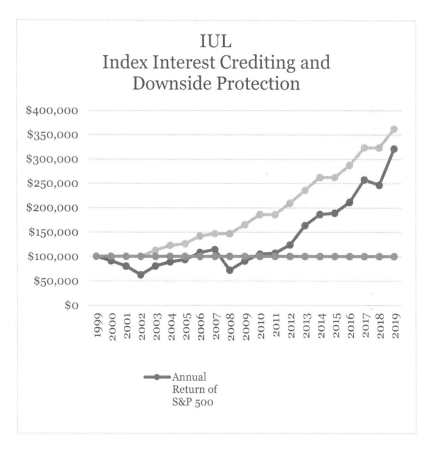

Preceding is a hypothetical illustration of the following:[45]

1. The top line, lightest in color, represents $100,000 used to purchase an IUL policy and allocated to an index interest crediting method tied to the performance of the S&P 500 index. It assumes a hypothetical cap rate of 12.5 percent and an interest rate floor of 0 percent.

2. The second, darkest line represents the S&P 500 index, including dividends.

3. The straight line represents the guaranteed interest rate floor.

Another opportunity IUL presents is for a policyholder to overfund the policy cash value in the first five or ten years and then, potentially, not have to pay any more money into the policy, letting the cash accumulation self-fund the policy. However, when overfunding an IUL policy, it is important to understand the policy may become a modified endowment contract (or MEC) if premium payments exceed certain amounts specified under the Internal Revenue Code. This can happen if a policy has been funded too quickly in its early years. For MECs, distributions during the life of the insured (including loans) are fully taxable as income to the extent there is a gain in the policy over the amount of net premiums paid. An additional 10 percent federal income tax may apply for withdrawals made before age fifty-nine-and-one-half.

So, back to our friend, Emma. If her permanent life insurance policy was an IUL, what might that have looked like? Emma saves, paying well over the mandatory minimum of her IUL policy. Let's assume the market does well for decades. Her policy accumulates a significant cash value. At some point, she stops paying as much in premium, or maybe she stops paying any premium from her own pocket at all because her policy has enough in cash value it is paying for its own expenses with the

[45] Standard & Poor's®, S&P® and S&P 500® are registered trademarks of Standard & Poor's Financial Services LLC. S&P 500® returns are based on information obtained from Yahoo Finance GSPC Historical Prices and StandardandPoors.com

insurance company. Then, when her brother needs help, there is enough cash value stored in the policy.

It's important to note that making withdrawals or taking policy loans from a policy may have an adverse effect. You may want to talk to your financial professional to re-evaluate your premium payment schedule if you are considering this option.

If you're reeling just a bit, it's understandable. There's a lot going on with these policies. If you don't take the time to understand the basics of how they work, it's entirely possible to fall behind on premium payments and end up with a policy that lapses. Yet, if you understand the terms of your contract and are working with purpose, an IUL could be a powerful cog in the greater mechanics of your overall retirement strategy.

In addition to the primary reason we purchase life insurance —the death benefit—I often encounter two additional primary applications for IUL, depending on where you are in life and what your goals are.

First, if you are younger and still accumulating wealth, an IUL can be a great tool for tax-free wealth. For example, I have an IUL that I contribute to annually. When my children are of age, I will access the available policy cash values via a loan to help pay for their college. Then I will continue to contribute to the policy until retirement, at which point I plan to draw the money out as another tax-free income source.

IUL policies are often a good fit for some of our clients as a tax-free retirement strategy, where we pull money out of pre-tax accounts, pay the tax, and then reposition the money inside of a tax-free IUL. This IUL can provide a tax-free income stream, which could offer a long-term care benefit or a legacy strategy of leaving more tax-free money to the next generation.

Of course, the policy needs to be carefully managed to ensure it is properly funded to remain in force. Loans will reduce the available cash values and death benefit and could cause the policy to lapse if it isn't monitored, It's important to work with your financial advisor to properly structure the policy.

Chapter 9: Indexed Universal Life Insurance
KEY CONCEPTS

✓ Like any permanent insurance, an IUL policy will remain in force as long as you continue to pay sufficient premiums.

✓ You can borrow against your policy's cash value, free of income tax

✓ Cash accumulation interest credits are based on an index, with what is called a "floor" and a "cap" or other limits such as a spread or participation rate.

Look Ahead. . .Chapter 10: Finding a Professional
Details behind my passion to help people capture as much wealth as possible while ensuring that their money doesn't run out in retirement

CHAPTER 10

Finding a Professional

"Before anything else, preparation is the key to success."
— *Alexander Graham Bell*

I didn't grow up thinking I'd become a lawyer or financial advisor. Like a lot of kids, my thing was sports, but as I grew older and entered college at Grand Valley State University, I decided I'd study psychology, like my father, who is a professor in that field. I was soon admitted to an honors program, and I began adding finance courses to my curriculum, which must have pleased my mother, as she holds an MBA in finance.

By graduating with dual degrees, one matching those possessed by each of my parents, it seemed I might follow their paths, had it not been for a particular undergraduate course.

As part of my finance track, I took a business law class and really knocked it out of the park. And even though I had received offers to work for several financial planning firms after graduation, my interest had been piqued. So I enrolled at The Michigan State University College of Law, where I graduated with a corporate concentration.

It was early days in my college career when I figured out that whatever my job would be, it had to be about helping others. By 2005 I finally had the education and training I needed to open my own law practice. Because my focus was estate planning, I soon learned that most of my clients were not nearly as concerned with death as they were with receiving adequate long-term care, which inspired me to become a Certified Elder Law Attorney® in 2008.

From the beginning, my passion has been about helping people capture as much wealth as possible while ensuring that their money doesn't run out in retirement. Helping clients accomplish both requires a truly holistic approach, so I decided to offer tax planning and preparation services as well.

Behind a great performance is a great coach

I grew up playing basketball, soccer, and tennis and feel fortunate to have been coached by my father. I may have never developed the skills to play professional sports, but without my dad, I wouldn't have improved as much as I did. Now, thirty years later, I'm coaching my own kids in soccer and watching them improve their skills and instincts.

All great athletes (I'm not placing myself in this category) achieved optimal levels of performance because an influential coach believed in their promise and potential to "do more." Tiger Woods, Serena Williams, Michael Jordan, Diana Taurasi, and Tom Brady have astonishing natural abilities. Still, they may have never been used in this example had it not been for Earl Woods, Richard Williams, Phil Jackson, Geno Auriemma, and Bill Belichick—coaches who knew how to get more from their incredible athletes.

These great coaches maximized abilities by using proven methods they developed to motivate numerous competitors. Their tactics gave athletes the ability to make sound decisions, while avoiding bad habits.

Players and coaches may share the goal of winning, but their jobs are very different. If Tom Brady had been born with Bill Belichick's knowledge and experience, he could have coached himself—truth is, after nineteen years under Belichick, he kind of did. After being named the national high school basketball player of the year, Diana Taurasi never stopped growing. She developed her abilities even more under Geno Auriemma and led UConn to three consecutive NCAA championships before her legendary WNBA career. Understanding the talent possessed by potential standouts and providing the instruction, encouragement, and discipline to help them grow into superstars is indicative of those who pour their passion into coaching.

I'm reminded of a conversation with a client before he decided to work with us. He was an engineer and had a natural inclination toward doing things for himself. But, like a lot of other smart people I'd worked with, he soon discovered that attempting to gain financial acumen can create a web of confusion, even for him.

One answered question can turn into three new ones. . .and on and on it can go. This gentleman didn't lack the intelligence or even the ability, but he did lack the experience.

For someone who has never worked in financial planning, the number of variables is overwhelming, but the interaction between those variables is when the snowball really gets rolling. Unless you committed to a financial planning career some time ago, it can be difficult to even know what your first question should be. For fifteen years, our firm has helped people figure out what the first question should be as well as pertinent follow-up questions.

Retirement is ever-changing. The answers to planning questions ten years ago frequently do not apply today. The old retirement paradigm, based on working one job that produced a lifetime pension after thirty years of service, now rarely applies. The new paradigm often includes frequent job changes, using 401ks or 403bs instead of pensions, and planning for more active years in retirement.

We recommend you review four aspects before committing to an advisor.

First, does the advisor provide services that pertain to *accumulation* or *preservation and distribution*? A lot of stockbrokers and advisors know a client's interest will be piqued if they talk about growing wealth, but growth can occur anyway when the markets are allowed to do what they do. Figuring out a plan for preservation and eventual distribution can be more complicated, and why you may need to partner with a skilled advisor.

Next, you need to determine if the advisor uses a holistic approach to planning. Independent advisors are likely to address the individual components that affect a larger overall financial plan. Some large brokerage houses and insurance firms use a "one size fits all" approach by offering only the products and tools they developed.

By working with a holistic company like ours, a larger toolbox is available to you. By putting together a Retirement & Legacy Blueprint™, we holistically structure an overall plan for income, investments, taxes, health care, and legacy—a far cry from individual products that tend to serve the best interest of a brokerage house.

The third element to look for is whether the advisor is a true fiduciary; meaning, is he/she legally bound to place your interest before their own? Not all financial professionals are fiduciaries—they may say they are, but don't be fooled. To help ensure sure inappropriate products with high fees are not being pushed on you, we suggest you work with an advisor legally bound to act in good faith.

As a fiduciary at Castle Wealth Group, I'm obligated to put your interests ahead of my own, which means I sit on the same side of the table when we plan your retirement and legacy.

Fourth, you need to find someone you trust. Retirement and legacy planning is a partnership between you and your advisor, and trusting that person is essential. Trust is perhaps most important when it comes to the care of a surviving spouse. You need to feel sure that your advisor will move forward with your plans when the time comes.

When you first meet an advisor, ask yourself these questions:

- How did they make you feel?
- Did they try to sell something to you?
- Are they a Certified Financial Planner™, or do they hold other similar retirement planning credentials?
- Do they seem credible?

If an advisor begins your first meeting by pitching a specific tool (such as an annuity), that should be a red flag. This kind of business practice could indicate that they are more concerned with sales than your best interests.

Our process always begins with listening and learning about you and what your goals are. Then (and only then) do we develop a strategy that identifies the appropriate tools to help you reach those goals.

Clarity, confidence, and comfort are key attributes we want you to feel after you have engaged in the process of developing your Retirement & Legacy Blueprint™.

Fees

Understanding how fees work is important, especially if you want to avoid falling prey to hidden or hard-to-understand ones. One way some companies charge fees is to tie them to your earnings as a ratio expense.

Working with other financial professionals and CPAs has given me a unique insight into the world of financial advice, and I haven't always liked what I've seen. During my first three years, I witnessed too many advisors who seemed to be acting in their own best interests instead of the best interests of their clients, which compelled me to add financial services to my practice.

The ethical and fiduciary responsibilities I'm bound to are tied to the licenses and certifications I hold. To remain in good standing as a practicing lawyer and financial advisor, I must adhere to stringent requirements pertaining to record-keeping, separation of funds, and many others. I'm also required to participate in state-mandated Continuing Education courses each year.

The credentials I've acquired mean a lot to me in terms of personal achievement, but they mean a lot to my clients too. Why? Because they represent a minimum threshold of ethical behavior and tells them I understand and follow the rules. Managing another person's wealth is serious business, and the overseers of this industry are serious about its professionals staying compliant.

Staying compliant is a big part of my job, but it's also what allows me to sleep at night. When I go to bed, I have to be able to honestly say to myself, "I put my client's first."

My legal education and experience have allowed me to understand complex legal structures (such as trusts, LLCs and other tax and legal entities). Coupling the law with my background in finance and psychology uniquely positions our firm to serve families who want to protect and preserve what they worked so hard to build.

Planning and managing your retirement and legacy is something we take seriously at Castle Wealth Group. The considerations I've outlined in this book are the tip of the iceberg, and so many more details must be addressed, but you do not have to do it alone. Our firm is here to help you customize a Retirement & Legacy Blueprint™ to help ensure your family is in the best possible position to manage preservation and distribution.

Your retirement and legacy are the culmination of every sacrifice and decision you've made up to this point. It represents day after day of hard work, getting up early to start a cold car in winter, and sacrificing the beach and golf in summer, while making sure your family had everything it needed. That is your retirement and legacy. I know how important it is to protect.

Acknowledgments

I'd like to first acknowledge my family for putting up with me.

Next, I wish to extend a warm thank you to our client family. When we onboard clients to our Retirement & Legacy Blueprint™, it doesn't take very long for us to feel connected to them. As we grow with them, we cheer for them in good times and experience their grief when loved ones are lost. I thank you for your continued support, and you are a part of our family.

I'd like to acknowledge and thank both the National Elder Law Foundation (NELF) and the National Academy of Elder Law Attorneys for organizing the stringent requirements and exams that allow those of us up to the task to become Certified Elder Law Attorneys (CELAs). The CELA® designation is often referred to as the "gold standard" for estate planning and elder law in the United States. When an advisor holds a CELA® designation, it helps clients understand that they are working with a professional dedicated to helping them protect everything they've worked so hard to earn.

Along those same lines, I must thank the Certified Financial Planner Board of Standards, which was instrumental in developing the idea of financial planning as a holistic approach rather than a "hot stock tip." The board's efforts are moving financial planning, as a profession, toward comprehensive approaches that combine income, investment, tax, health care, and legacy planning. Thank you to the CFP® board for creating a designation that seeks to distinguish true financial planning from selling stocks, annuities, or insurance.

About the Author

Christopher J. Berry

Christopher J. Berry, Esq., JD, CELA®, CFP®, and Castle Wealth Group is focused on helping clients reach their post-career goals by offering them a well-thought-out strategy for retirement and legacy planning.

Chris began in 2005 as an estate-planning attorney before adding elder law, tax services, and financial services to his practice in 2008.

He truly enjoys helping families plan, protect, and preserve what they've worked so hard for. He developed the Retirement

& Legacy Blueprint™ to help families align their income, investment, tax, health care, and legacy goals into one effective comprehensive plan.

Chris serves clients in Michigan and across the country, and holds insurance licenses in Michigan, South Carolina, Florida and Georgia. He is a practicing attorney and holds a Series 65 license as a registered investment adviser representative.

Chris has served as a paid instructor to attorneys, financial advisors and CPAs, offering continued education both locally and nationally. He has been an adjunct professor of law at Western Michigan University's Cooley Law School. Castle Wealth Group has been recognized as a model firm by the Institute of Continued Legal Education. Chris' articles have been featured in Forbes, Kiplinger's, and Yahoo Finance. Chris' previous book is titled, *The Caregiver's Legal Guide to Planning for a Loved one With Chronic Illness*.

He earned degrees in Finance and Psychology from Grand Valley State University and a law degree from Michigan State University College of Law.

Chris enjoys spending time with his wife Rochelle and his kids, Ryan and Madison. Chris also enjoys grilling on his Traeger Grill, doing CrossFit, Brazilian Jiu-Jitsu, and telling bad dad jokes to make his kids laugh.

BRIGHTON
1024 E. Grand River Ave., Suite A
Brighton, Michigan 48116

Phone
844.885.4200

Web
CastleWealthGroup.com
MichiganEstatePlanning.com

Made in the USA
Middletown, DE
20 April 2023

29174952R00082